O'BRIEN POCKET HISTORY OF

GAELIC SPORTS

**A history of and guide to the sports of the
Gaelic Athletic Association.**

Gaelic football, hurling, camogie and handball are the
traditional sports of Ireland. Since 1884, under the aegis
of the Gaelic Athletic Association (GAA), Gaelic sports,
particularly football and hurling, have been hugely
popular. County rivalry is as passionate today as it ever
was and it is the ambition of every player to represent
their county in Croke Park. This is a concise and lively
account of the games and the players, the teams and the
history of Gaelic sports.

EAMONN SWEENEY is a sports writer, novelist and playwright. An avid sports fan, he has written about Gaelic sports for the *Irish Examiner* and *Sunday Independent*. He is the author of the bestselling *Munster Hurling Legends* and *The Road to Croker*, and a regular contributor to TV and radio sports programmes. He lives in West Cork.

Other books by Eamonn Sweeney

Munster Hurling Legends, Seven Decades of the Greatest Teams, Players and Games

O'BRIEN POCKET HISTORY OF

Gaelic Sports

Eamonn Sweeney

THE O'BRIEN PRESS
DUBLIN

DEDICATION
To Maura

First published 2004 by The O'Brien Press Ltd,
20 Victoria Road, Dublin 6, Ireland.
Tel: +353 1 4923333; Fax: +353 1 4922777
E-mail: books@obrien.ie
Website: www.obrien.ie

ISBN: 0-86278-854-4

British Library Cataloguing-in-Publication Data
A catalogue record for this title is available from the British Library.

1 2 3 4 5 6 7 8 9 10
04 05 06 07 08 09

Editing, typesetting, layout and design: The O'Brien Press Ltd
Printing: Cox & Wyman Ltd

Contents

1. THE EVOLUTION OF GAELIC SPORTS

Irish people have always had a natural love of games and gambling on games, and Gaelic sports can boast an ancient lineage. The very fact of being called *Gaelic* games invokes the Pre-Christian era, a claim not altogether false. Of the four sports dealt with here – hurling, football, camogie and handball – hurling can lay the strongest claim to being an ancient game.

There is a reference in the Book of Leinster, written in the twelfth century, to a game of hurling at the Battle of Moytura in 1272BC between the Tuatha Dé Danann and the Firbolgs, two legendary fearsome tribes said to be sworn rivals. Following the game, the Firbolgs slew their opponents – a bloodthirsty action many might feel to be entirely in keeping with the passions hurling provokes. Hurling plays an important role in much of the legend and folklore of Ireland. For instance, the mighty Cúchulainn was said to puck a *sliotar* along as he travelled, to have outclassed all opponents on the field of play, and to have once killed a ferocious hound by thrusting his *sliotar* down its throat.

There is also a reference to hurling in the Brehon Laws, and in the Statutes of Kilkenny (1366) and of Galway (1537) members of the Anglo-Irish ruling class were expressly forbidden to play it – as part of the general drive to prevent them from becoming Gaelicised, or 'going native'. These interdictions had little effect, however, and the game flourished under the aegis of landlords who would organise teams of their tenants to play inter-barony and inter-county matches on which a great deal of money was wagered.

Football is not as ancient a sport as hurling, but an early form of it, called *Caid* – in which a community 'team' would try to bring a ball as far as a neighbouring village and the neighbouring villagers would do everything in their power to prevent them doing so – had been played for centuries.

However, things changed as Irish history took some

dramatic twists and turns. The 1798 rebellion led to a cooling of relations between landlords and tenants, and in the following century the Great Famine had a disastrous effect on native Irish culture. By the mid-nineteenth century, both hurling and football, like the Irish language, were in decline. It looked as though the great native sports would shortly become extinct and be superseded by games imported from England. The inevitable was thwarted, however, by the nationalist fervour and missionary zeal of a group of men who together founded the Gaelic Athletic Association, or the GAA. Their passion for the sports of Ireland proved a catalyst, and would result in the games not only being saved from extinction but being promoted to a level those men could only have dreamed of.

2. THE ORIGINS OF THE GAA

Cumann Lúthchleas Gael, or the Gaelic Athletic Association, was a nationalist organisation from the outset. Its formation was contemporaneous with that of the Gaelic League, and like the League it was a product of the cultural nationalism of the time – it was no coincidence that hurleys were carried as substitutes for guns on ceremonial occasions, for example, Charles Stewart Parnell's funeral. The Gaelic Athletic Association was very much a creature of the political ferment of the late nineteenth century, which would eventually lead to the Easter Rising and Irish Independence in 1922.

Its inception was due to a brilliant, enthusiastic, sometimes fanatical and undeniably difficult man: Michael Cusack. He was a school teacher from Clare who lived in Dublin and was a member of the Irish Republican Brotherhood (IRB); Cusack became familiar to many through his characterisation as the Citizen, a zealous nationalist, in James Joyce's *Ulysses*. In an article in the *United Irishman* newspaper, Cusack called for the setting up of a national sporting body to preserve the traditional games of the country. The first meeting of this body was called for 1 November 1884 in the billiards room of Hayes's Commercial Hotel, Thurles, in County Tipperary.

It was an inauspicious beginning for such a remarkable organisation. The minutes of the meeting record the names of just seven attendees – although another six men sometimes claimed to have been present. The seven who did turn up were: Michael Cusack, Maurice Davin, John Wyse-Power, John McKay, JK Bracken, Joseph O'Ryan and Thomas St George McCarthy, and in all likelihood they did not know what they were starting. The GAA entered the world not with a bang but with a barely audible whimper.

The founders were a mixed bunch. Davin, a Carrick-on-Suir man, was probably the best-known of them as he was one of the leading athletes of the day. Wyse-Power was editor of the *Leinster Leader* and a member of the IRB. McCarthy, on the other hand, was a Tipperary man who was a District Inspector in the Royal Irish Constabulary, the police force of the British authorities in Ireland. Bracken was a building contractor from Templemore, O'Ryan was a solicitor from Carrick-on-Suir and McKay was a journalist from Belfast who was working for the *Cork Examiner*.

The new body elected to invite appropriate persons to be patrons of the organisation. They approached Dr Thomas Croke, the Archbishop of Cashel, Michael Davitt and Charles Stewart Parnell. While Parnell and Davitt had little to do with the rise of the GAA, the energetic and inspiring Dr Croke proved an excellent choice. His letter of acceptance to the Board was regarded as an unofficial charter for the GAA. Its fiery nationalist rhetoric gives some idea of the heady atmosphere in which the GAA was conceived:

> 'We are daily importing from England, not only her manufactured goods, which we cannot help doing, since she has practically strangled our own manufacturing appliances, but, together with her fashions, her

accents, her vicious literature, her music, her dances and her manifold mannerisms, her games also and her pastimes, to the utter discredit of our own grand national sports and to the sore humiliation, as I believe, of every genuine son and daughter of our old land. Ball-playing, hurling, football-kicking, according to Irish rules, casting, leaping in various ways, wrestling, handy-grips, top-pegging, leap-frog, rounders, tip-in-the-hat and all the favourite exercises and amusements among men and boys may now be said to be not only dead and buried but in several localities to be entirely forgotten and unknown ... Indeed, if we keep travelling for the next score years in the same direction that we have been going in for some time past, condemning the sports that were practised by our forefathers, effacing our national features as though we were ashamed of them and putting on, with England's stuffs and broadcloths, her masher habits and such other effeminate follies that she may recommend, we had better, at once and publicly abjure our nationality, clap hands for joy at the sight of the Union Jack and place 'England's bloody red' exultantly above the green.'

Sadly, the wonderfully named handy-grips, tip-in-the-hat and top-pegging never did regain their past eminence, but the GAA made a huge impact with football and hurling. This was not due to sharp insight on the Board's part; initially the main aim of Cusack and his cohorts was to take over athletics, hence the organisation's name. They did this to some degree, but it soon became apparent that hurling and football outstripped athletics in popularity, and the GAA eventually farmed out its athletics events to a separate organisation, the National Athletics and Cycling Association (NACA), which dwindled in influence before being subsumed by the more powerful Bord Lúthchleas na hÉireann (BLE) in the 1990s.

The Association also showed that it was in tune with the tenor of the times by undergoing a rancorous split early in its existence. Less than two years after the Thurles meeting, Cusack fell out with Croke and also incurred the wrath of the GAA in Cork. Wyse-Power engineered the removal of Cusack as Secretary, and the man who had started it all found himself out in the cold. Like Parnell after him in the political sphere, he found it impossible to regain his influence in the organisation he had pioneered. Two years later, Davin resigned as President after another dispute and Wyse-Power quit shortly after that.

Despite the internal conflict, the GAA quickly gained a reputation for being well run and it wasn't long before it could lay claim to being the leading sporting organisation in the country. The attractiveness of the games of hurling and football and the opportunity they gave for the expression of local pride were huge factors in this, but the efficiency of the Association had a lot to do with it too. It spread the revived games all over the country and by 1887 – just three years after its inception – was able to organise the first ever All-Ireland Football and Hurling Championships. The finals, which weren't played until April 1888, were contested by club teams from the counties involved – a pattern which continued until 1922 when the hurling final between Kilkenny and Tipperary was the first contested by two county selections. Back in 1888, Limerick, represented by Commercials, played in the football final, held in Clonskeagh, against Louth, represented by Dundalk Young Irelands. Limerick won 1-4 to 0-3. The hurling final was played in Birr, County Offaly, and was won by Tipperary (Thurles) who beat Galway (Meelick) 1-1 to 0-0. The different mores of the era are apparent when you consider that the Meelick players, thinking the team from Thurles would not turn up as they were late arriving, went to the pub instead, only to find that the game would be taking place after all. The fact that they didn't score at all can be easily explained, it would seem. And that wasn't the only striking difference: one Meelick player, John Lowry, had walked all the way to Birr only to find he was on the substitutes' bench. Understandably perhaps, he refused to accept this decision and periodically went onto the field to help out his team-mates, regardless of the fact that they had the requisite number of players as it was. The teams played in their shirts and trousers. It was a basic enough start, but the GAA was on the move.

Playing with Pride

This book deals with the two major sports of Gaelic football and hurling, as well as handball and camogie – relatively minor but nonetheless important games organised by the GAA. The common thread that runs through all these games is that they are a means of expressing local pride. Players don't go into the fray year after year for money, they do it for their club and their county. This is a defining characteristic of Gaelic sports. Throughout the twentieth century Irish people often needed an outlet, a reason to feel proud, to feel bonded as a community – beset on all sides by economic woes, religious repression and political conservatism, sport was the most immediate means of providing a sense of unfettered joy. And the GAA was the conduit for this good feeling, something the organisation recognised and encouraged.

From the start the GAA made use of the great local pride in Irish society. Clubs were generally organised on a parish basis and the championships were contested between county teams. Players, with a few exceptions, played for the parish or county where they were born and bred, and would spend their whole career with the same club. This gave a unique intensity to local rivalries and endowed the best counties with a powerful, long-standing tradition. For instance, Kerry emerged as the undisputed kings of Gaelic football, while the Big Three of Tipperary, Cork and Kilkenny have long dominated hurling. But the victory wreaths have been passed around and only three counties – Westmeath, Wicklow and Fermanagh – have never won a senior provincial title. The championship is further divided into four provincial sections – Connacht, Ulster, Munster and Leinster – adding another layer of rivalry that exploits the natural seam of inter-province one-upmanship. Indeed, the Munster hurling final is almost as prestigious an event as the All-Ireland final, with teams playing for their lives in an attempt to lord it over old enemies. The most famous, and most enduring, rivalries include Kilkenny–Wexford and Cork–Tipperary in hurling, and Kerry–Cork, Dublin–Meath and Galway–Mayo in football. When these teams line up against each other, the tension levels are enough to make the hairs stand up on the back of your neck.

Perhaps it was the GAA's appeal to local pride that ensured it was so firmly rooted in Irish society that even when the country changed dramatically in other ways, Gaelic games remained as strong as ever. The games draw huge crowds, with All-Ireland championship attendances up there with those of the Champions League. Put that in the context of Ireland's relatively small population and it's obvious that the GAA is intertwined with Irish communities in a way unmatched by any other sporting organisation in Europe. No part of Ireland is untouched by the Championship Summer. In the end, you don't really know Ireland if you don't know the GAA.

The GAA off the field

Around the turn of the last century provincial structures were established and the number of counties participating in the championships increased greatly. Organisation improved to the extent that the 1909 hurling final was the first decider to be played in its designated year.

The GAA managed to continue in operation throughout the years of the War of Independence (1919–1921) and the Civil

War (1922–1923). The bitter political climate of the times did not seem to affect the Association, though there were occasional controversies, for example, Kerry withdrew from the championship as late as 1935 in protest against the treatment of republican prisoners by the Fianna Fáil government of the day. But these were only minor setbacks. Overall, the GAA took the new century by the horns and worked tirelessly to promote the games, and the organisation, in every corner of Ireland.

William Clifford, President of the GAA from 1926 to 1928, spoke of his hope of seeing 'a field in every parish', and this far-sighted GAA policy was put into effect to such an extent that by the 1960s every county had at least one ground capable of hosting big matches. In this respect, perhaps the key figure in the modernisation of the GAA was Pádraig Ó Caoimh, who had served time in jail for republican activities during the War of Independence and who served as General Secretary of the GAA from 1929 to 1964. Born in Roscommon but brought up in Cork, Ó Caoimh was a hugely able administrator. He was instrumental in the development of Croke Park and in the implementation of Clifford's grounds programme; the GAA was unrivalled in its ability to provide grounds and facilities in the smallest of villages and towns. The Association further strengthened this policy in the 1960s with the establishment of committees to disburse grants to clubs which were trying to develop their own grounds. The result is that clubs from some of the smallest parishes in the country play at grounds with fine dressing rooms for the players and stands for the spectators. In some ways this is the GAA's most impressive achievement.

That is not to suggest that it has all been plain sailing off the field for the GAA. For many people, The Ban is the great black mark against the Association's name. The Ban, or Rule 27, which was introduced in 1902, forbade GAA members to play, attend, or promote rugby, hockey, soccer, or cricket, ie, 'foreign games', under pain of suspension from the Association. Whatever sense it made during a time of resurgent cultural and political nationalism, The Ban seemed a stubborn anachronism in a newly independent Ireland, and there were attempts to have it abolished at the GAA Congresses of 1923, 1924 and 1925.

Nevertheless, Rule 27 stayed and became a source of much bitterness. In 1938, for example, the GAA removed Dr Douglas Hyde, President of Ireland, as patron because in his capacity as President he had attended a soccer match. This was a good example of the venality of the Rule's supporters. Not alone could GAA members be banned because they had played soccer or rugby but they could also be suspended merely for attending functions organised by those sporting clubs. Such a fate befell the legendary Waterford hurler Tom Cheasty in 1963 when he was denied the chance of playing in a National Hurling League final because he had attended a soccer-club dance.

A distasteful side-effect of The Ban's continuance was the setting up of Vigilance Committees, whose members had the job of attending rugby and soccer matches to check if any other GAA members were present, and reporting them. The enlisting of Association members as spies and tattle-tales was perhaps the sorriest thing ever done in the name of the GAA. The Ban was finally abolished in 1971 at a Congress in Belfast and its demise, as had long been argued, had no detrimental effect on the GAA. It had simply been a case of ill-founded cultural paranoia.

There was another Rule which got the GAA into hot water. Rule 21 banned members of the British Army or the RUC (Royal Ulster Constabulary, the former police force of Northern Ireland) from joining the Association, an action that was far more serious than The Ban and one for which the arguments for and against were much less clear-cut. On the one hand was the fact that during the Troubles in Northern Ireland few Catholics regarded Army or RUC personnel as anything other than servants of the British government and the Protestant community. The GAA drew almost all of its members in the North from the Catholic community, and therefore had little option but to continue with the Rule or face the wrath of their Catholic members. The organisation came under fierce criticism for doing so, as Rule 21 was obviously far from compatible with the integrationist policies being put forward by Northern Irish, Irish and British political parties seeking to bring peace to Northern Ireland. It was frequently repeated by Unionist politicians that Rule 21 was 'sectarian', an allegation that was still being levelled at the organisation when a Protestant, Jack Boothman of Wicklow, was President of the Association in the 1990s.

Some GAA members argued for the abolition of the Rule in the interests of reconciliation, but attitudes were hardened by what was seen as the harassment of Association members by the security forces. British soldiers occupied part of the Crossmaglen Rangers' football grounds in Armagh, an action that was hugely controversial and provoked tempers and arguments. Likewise, a tragic incident when Aidan McAnespie was shot dead by a British soldier as he walked across the border on his way to a football match was hugely significant in terms of the ongoing debate.

Pressure for abolition grew when ceasefires were declared in the North in the 1990s, and by 1998 Rule 21 appeared ready to go. Instead, Congress hedged its bets and decided that the Rule would be abolished only when a police service acceptable to the Northern Catholic population was put in place. This happened in 2001 when the RUC was replaced by the Police Service of Northern Ireland (PSNI), which in turn meant the abolition of Rule 21 was now inevitable. Even so, Down was the only one of the Six Counties to vote in favour of removing the Rule.

The organisation of the GAA

The GAA is organised in four tiers: national level, provincial level, county level and club level. The clubs are the basic unit of the organisation.

National level

At national level the GAA is run by Central Council, with the Management Committee in charge of the day-to-day functions of the organisation. These bodies run the All-Ireland stages of the inter-county and inter-club championships and the Railway Cup. They also implement rule changes and amendments to GAA structures; major changes must be ratified by these bodies.

The rank-and-file of the GAA have their chance to air their opinions at the annual National Congress, at which delegates from all County Boards present motions which have been passed at their County Conventions. Proposed changes to the rules of the games require a two-thirds majority in order to be passed. There can be tension between Central Council and Congress on some issues. For example, it is widely held that senior officials of the Association would like to make Croke Park available for use by other sporting bodies, but are stymied by their inability to get a vote to this effect passed at Congress. Indeed, votes on the matter of Croke Park usually take the form of a motion proposing that Central Council be allowed to make decisions on individual applications, judging each case on its own merits without having to refer it back to Congress. Special Congresses can be held on matters of extreme controversy.

A President of the GAA is elected every three years. The current incumbent is Sean Kelly of Kerry, the first man from his county to hold the office. Former playing greats, such as Donal Keenan of Roscommon, Alf Murray of Armagh and Paddy Buggy of Kilkenny, have all held the office. Notable past presidents include William Clifford of Limerick (the great apostle of grounds development), Pat Fanning of Waterford (who presided over the removal of The Ban) and Peter Quinn (a prime mover behind the creation of the ultra-modern new Croke Park stadium).

Presidents can also overstep the mark occasionally. John Dowling of Offaly landed himself in hot water by criticising the tactics of the Meath team in the 1987 All-Ireland final replay. Similarly, Jack Boothman of Wicklow might have been better off not berating the defeated Limerick team for their performance in the 1996 All-Ireland hurling final, while the thoroughly decent Joe McDonagh of Galway pledged to remove Rule 21, but found this impossible to achieve during his tenure.

The General Secretary of the GAA has a greater effect on the Association than the President, partly because these officials tend to stay in office for many years. Pádraig Ó Caoimh, for example, who held the post from 1929 to 1964, was hugely influential in the modernising of the Association. And the current General Secretary, Liam Mulvihill of Longford, was a driving force behind the redevelopment of Croke Park and is viewed as an eminently able power behind the throne.

Though they are within the ambit of the GAA, camogie, handball and ladies' football all have their own national governing bodies.

Provincial level

The four Provincial Councils organise the Provincial Championships for clubs and counties and administer disciplinary matters in their jurisdiction. A win in the provincial football championships guarantees entry to the All-Ireland quarter-finals. There isn't such a level playing field in hurling, however. While a win in the Munster and Leinster hurling championships guarantees entry to the All-Ireland semi-finals, Connacht and Ulster are considerably weaker in hurling and therefore don't enjoy such a privilege. Galway, as the only strong Connacht team, are automatically entered into the knockout stages. The Ulster champions enter at the same point in the competition.

County level

The thirty-two County Boards organise GAA affairs within their own county borders. There are also separate boards which organise under-age competitions. In the larger counties, the County Board is subdivided into divisional boards for different areas. The annual County Convention elects officials, deals with motions regarding the running of the GAA within the county and also motions with a national application which, if passed, go forward to Congress.

Club level

The fundamental unit of the GAA is the club, of which there are over 2,500 in Ireland. Clubs are usually organised on a parish basis, though some may be a combination of parishes, while larger parishes may have more than one club. There are also extra-parochial clubs, such as those affiliated from third-level educational institutions, or the Garda club in Dublin. Clubs hold an AGM to elect officers and to send motions to the County Convention, which might make it all the way to Congress.

The future of the Association

The GAA has, if anything, grown stronger in recent years and prophecies of doom about the effect of soccer and rugby on the Association have been proven wrong. The most potent symbol of the organisation's current strength is the new-look Croke Park. In 1993 an immensely ambitious programme for the redevelopment of the stadium got underway, and ten years later the gates swung open to reveal the new face of the GAA in Ireland. Instrumental in this were the then President of the GAA, Peter Quinn from Armagh, and the General Secretary, Liam Mulvihill. It was a bold plan, but it paid dividends. Croke Park was transformed almost beyond recognition into one of the finest stadia in Europe. It now stands as a monument to an Association whose progress from humble beginnings has been one of the great success stories of Irish life.

Rules 21 and 27 may be gone, but a few controversies remain to trouble the minds of GAA administrators. The first is the question of whether 'foreign games', specifically soccer, should be allowed to be played in Croke Park. A motion that would have led to this being permitted was defeated by the narrowest of margins in 2001. Since then the GAA has come under increasing pressure to open the gates of its flagship stadium to other sports, especially as the national soccer team have no ground to call their own. The issue is delicately poised at the moment, with senior administrators and a majority of players probably in favour of sharing Croke Park, but delegates to the County Boards and Congress seemingly against the change. Which way the wind blows on this issue in the next few years is anyone's guess.

The subject of professionalism has also reared its head in recent years. Amateurism has always been one of the core values of the GAA and always made sound economic sense. But lately, with the new Croke Park drawing huge ticket-and merchandise-buying crowds and an increase in the number of professional administrators being employed by the Association, players have begun to question the lack of financial rewards they receive from their participation in the games. This concern led to the setting up of the Gaelic Players' Association (GPA) in 1999. The GAA at first refused to deal with the GPA and set up its own players' body, but the GPA has gone from strength to strength and is now regarded as the representative organisation for players.

The GPA floated a proposal that players be paid €127 per week during the playing season, but the GAA dismissed this as impractical. There has been an improvement in the treatment of players with regard to expenses and fringe benefits, such as free gym membership, but the players want to see more concrete changes made and a greater understanding of the issues they are voicing. Dissatisfaction on this score led to the unprecedented decision by the Cork senior hurling panel to go on strike in 2002. That dispute was settled quickly, but the bigger issue of player compensation is far from being resolved.

3. THE MAJOR GAA COMPETITIONS

Obviously the biggest competitions and prizes in the GAA are the All-Ireland Championships and the Sam Maguire and Liam McCarthy Cups. Played in September each year, the All-Ireland is the dream win of all teams, securing them a place in the pantheon of greatest players. Unlike other modern sports, these men do not compete for money or fame, they are driven by pride in their counties and clubs and passion for the games they love. In football, they compete for what is probably the most famous sports trophy in Ireland: the Sam Maguire. The Cup was first presented at the 1928 final in which Kildare beat Cavan. Sam Maguire, a Protestant from the Dunmanway area of Cork, had been Chief Intelligence Officer in the Irish Republican Brotherhood (he initiated Michael Collins into the movement) and had played for London in the 1901 All-Ireland football final against Cork. For the hurlers, it is the Liam McCarthy Cup they want to hold aloft on All-Ireland day. It was first presented at the 1921 final in which Limerick beat Dublin. Liam McCarthy was born in London of a Cork father and a Limerick mother and was involved in the GAA in Britain for many years. There is a network of associated competitions which feed into the All-Ireland heart of the games, and these are described below.

National Leagues
The inaugural National Leagues took place in 1926 and have afforded followers of football and hurling some spectacular

moments. The Leagues run from March to May, the All-Ireland Championships from May to September. (The months from September to March are taken up with club competitions.) Second only to the All-Ireland Championships in prestige, the National Leagues have lost a lot of their lustre in recent years. For many years a National League title was considered a major honour, but increasing concentration on the championship has seen this secondary competition relegated to a sideshow.

But there is life in the old dog yet. In the past few years the League season has begun in February rather than October, a move that seems to have reawakened spectator interest. Plus, the 2003 All-Ireland champions, Tyrone and Kilkenny, both scooped the League title first, a fact that may well lead county managers to rethink their attitude towards the competition.

There have been many changes over the years to the structure of the hurling and football Leagues, but the basic model is: teams are streamed into divisions and play on a league basis, with the best sides going on to a knockout stage. One notable innovation in the football National League occurred from 1950 to 1952 and again from 1963 to 1969 (1970 in the case of hurling), when New York secured automatic passage to the final in an effort to promote the game in America. The winners of the 'Home Final', as it was known, met New York, generally playing two games, one at home and one in New York. The New York team actually won the 1950 and 1967 National Football Leagues, defeating Cavan and Galway respectively. Unfortunately, the experiment was discontinued after referee Clem Foley was assaulted following the 1970 Hurling League final between Cork and New York. Twenty years later it was revived for one year, with Kilkenny defeating New York in the hurling final and Cork beating them in the football final.

As expected, Kerry have won the most National Football League titles, with sixteen to their credit thus far. Surprisingly, Mayo are in second place with eleven titles – compared to just three in the All-Ireland Championship. This rating is largely due to their wonderful team of the 1930s, which won six League titles in a row between 1934 and 1939, a record that will probably never be broken. Longford is a small but football-mad midland county, and can lay claim to just one National League title, but it's a notable one. In the 1966 National League they defeated Galway in the 'Home Final' and New York in the final proper – a moment of glory that can still bring a tear to a Longford man's eye. The record-winning margin in a League final is the twenty points by which Kerry (4-16) beat Derry (1-5) in the 1961 decider.

Kerry's formidable team of the late 1920s and early 1930s won a four-in-a-row between 1928 and 1931, a feat matched by a later Kingdom team, which won between 1971 and 1974. However, it indicates the changing priorities of inter-county managers that the magnificent Kerry team of 1975–1986 won just three National League football titles in their eleven-year career, in 1975, 1982 and 1984. Achieving the double whammy of the National League and All-Ireland titles is the dream of every team, but it takes a truly gifted team to secure that ideal. Kerry did it in 1929, 1930, 1931 and 1984; Mayo in 1936; Cavan in 1948; Dublin in 1958; Kerry in 1959; Down in 1960; Galway in 1965; Down in 1968; Dublin in 1976; Kerry in 1984; Meath in 1988; Cork in 1989; Kerry in 1997; and Tyrone in 2003.

While the major counties can sometimes seem to treat National League success lightly, the competition has provided great days for football's lesser lights. There was wild jubilation in 1985 when Monaghan beat Armagh in the final to win their first national title. That League victory remains a red-letter day in Monaghan GAA history as the county has yet to win a senior championship, something which can also be said of Laois, who won a memorable final against Monaghan in 1986. Derry were the League specialists in the 1990s, winning three titles and adding a further one in 2000, but they now seem to have been succeeded by neighbours Tyrone, who took the 2002 and 2003 National League titles.

In hurling the Big Three are not quite as dominant in the National League as they are in the championship. True, Tipperary leads the way with eighteen titles and Cork are in second with fourteen, but Kilkenny, on eleven, shares third place with Limerick. The great Limerick hurling team of the 1930s had a remarkably similar record to the Mayo football team of that time, winning five in a row from 1934 to 1938. Like the football competition the hurling League was suspended from 1942 to 1945 due to wartime transport restrictions. When it resumed in 1946, Clare won a rare national crown against Dublin.

Tipperary gained a reputation as League specialists when they won nine of the thirteen titles on offer from 1949 to 1961. They also won the infamous 1968 league final against Kilkenny, which included several bouts of fisticuffs between the teams, resulted in lengthy suspensions being handed down and led the Tipperary County Board to impose a media ban because newspaper reporters had reported the evidence of their own eyes. Tipp were again involved in the 1975 final, a much more edifying occasion with Galway announcing their revival by winning 4-9 to 4-6 in a memorable thriller.

A Clare team which flattered only to deceive in the championship had the consolation of putting the county back on the hurling map in 1977 and 1978 with League final victories over Kilkenny. And perhaps the most remarkable hurling League final of all was the 1993 contest, which went to a second replay before Cork finally saw off the challenge of a Wexford team seeking its first national title in twenty years.

Kilkenny have won both the All-Ireland Championship and the National League titles for the last two years (2002 and 2003). The double was also achieved by Cork in 19`6, Kilkenny in 1933, Limerick in 1934 and 1936, Cork in 19`1, Tipperary in 1949 and 1950, Cork in 1953, Wexford in 1956, Tipperary in 1961, 1964 and 1965, Cork in 1970, Kilkenny in 1982 and 1983,

Galway in 1987 and Tipperary in 2001. The record-winning margin in a decider is the twenty-one points by which Tipperary (6-14) beat New York (2-5) in the 1952 final.

The Railway Cup

It's hard to think of a sporting competition anywhere which has suffered such a reversal of fortune as the Railway Cup. Once a highly prestigious competition which drew huge crowds on St Patrick's Day, it is now played in front of miniscule audiences and evokes very little interest. Why this happened is something of a mystery, but the Cup has certainly been supplanted in the public's affections by the club championships, which have taken its old 17 March berth. Yet the old competition lingers on with the finals of 2003 being played in Rome – to reward the persevering players with a trip abroad. It probably drew a better crowd there than it would have attracted at home.

It was not always thus. The Railway Cup matches were once fiercely competitive and were especially valued for giving players from weaker counties a chance on the national stage. Kildare's Pat Dunny and Laois's Christy O'Brien in hurling, and Derry's Sean O'Connell and Sligo's Mickey Kearins in football are notable examples of this. They also enabled the game's greats to shine: Christy Ring played forty-four games in the competition and won eighteen, from 1942 to 1963, scoring a total of forty-two goals and 104 points in the process. He won his last Railway Cup medal when he was forty-three years old. The record attendance for a hurling final is 49,000 for the 1954 match, in which Leinster beat Munster 0-9 to 0-5.

The first Railway Cup competitions were held in 1927, with Munster winning the football title and Leinster the hurling title. Both results were slightly misleading as to the subsequent course of events. Leinster dominated the football competition in its early years, winning five of the six titles between 1928 and 1933. Connacht's golden era followed, with titles in 1934, 1936, 1937 and 1938. Oddly, considering their later dominance, Ulster did not win their first Railway Cup until 1942, when they defeated Munster by 1-10 to 1-5.

Leinster set a new record for consecutive wins with a four-in-a-row from 1952 to 1955, a mark which was equalled by Ulster between 1963 and 1966. The record was matched again by Leinster between 1985 and 1988, before finally being broken by Ulster who put together a superb six-in-a-row between 1989 and 1995 (the competition was not held in 1990). Quite rightly, Ulster holds the most football titles.

Memorable Railway Cup football finals include Ulster's breakthrough victory in 1942 when the quick handpassing of an Ulster team inspired by the great Kevin Armstrong of Antrim was too much for a Munster team composed almost entirely of Kerrymen. And Ulster's 3-7 to 2-9 win over Munster is reputed to have been the most exciting Railway Cup final ever, with Armagh's Alf Murray getting the winning point late in the game. Ulster's 3-11 to 2-11 victory over Connacht in 1973 was notable because it earned Sean O'Neill a record eighth medal, while Jimmy Barry-Murphy's four-goal haul as Munster beat Ulster 6-7 to 0-15 stands as one of the greatest individual feats in the competition's history.

An unusual name appears on the football roll of honour – Combined Universities – which won the title in 1973, one of two years in which the colleges competed.

Leinster's best run in the Railway Cup came between 1971 and 1975 when they won five in a row. From 1980 onwards Connacht became a force to be reckoned with in the competition and they were the dominant province in the 1980s with six wins. Ulster has yet to win a Railway Cup in hurling, though they came agonisingly close in 1995 when losing the final 0-13 to 1-9 to Munster.

The story of the Railway Cup in hurling, however, has been largely one of Munster dominance, especially in the early years of the competition, and Munster currently holds the most titles. From 1937 to 1953, a golden era of Munster hurling which included the heyday of Christy Ring and Mick Mackey, Munster won fifteen of the seventeen Railway Cups. A notable interruption came in 1947 when Connacht, or Galway as the team actually was and has remained with a few exceptions, beat them by 2-5 to 1-1. The run included a six-in-a-row between 1948 and 1953, which remains a Railway Cup record.

All-Ireland Minor Championship

The All-Ireland Minor Championship features the youngest competitive players of the games: players must be under eighteen years of age on 1 January of the year of the competition. The finals are played on All-Ireland day each year, and have provided many memorable curtain-raisers for the primary attraction – the Senior Cup Final. The first Minor Championship in football kicked off in 1929, with Clare clinching the title, while its hurling counterpart preceded it by a year, with Dublin being crowned the 1928 champs.

Kerry are the kingpins of minor football with eleven titles, closely followed by Cork and Dublin with ten apiece. All three counties have achieved a three-in-a-row: Kerry from 1931 to 1933; Cork from 1967 to 1969; and Dublin from 1954 to 1956. Perhaps the most notable final was in 1995 when Westmeath won their first ever All-Ireland football title by defeating Derry 1-10 to 0-11, a result which sparked scenes of celebration that almost overshadowed the senior match.

The Big Three have been their usual dominant selves in minor hurling, with Cork and Kilkenny at the top of the pile with eighteen titles each and Tipperary just behind. Once more the record is three in a row, achieved by Cork from 1937 to 1939 and again from 1969 to 1971, Kilkenny from 1960 to 1962 and Tipperary from 1932 to 1934 and from 1955 to 1957. Tipp's record in the 1950s deserves special mention as they won six of the eight titles available between 1952 and 1959.

Cork achieved the double at minor level in 1967, 1969 and 1974. Dublin managed the same feat in 1945 and 1954. The coveted treble of senior, under-21 and minor titles in the same year has been achieved just once in football, by Kerry in 1975, and three times in hurling, by Cork in 1970 and Kilkenny in 1975 and 2003.

Under-21 Championship

The All-Ireland under-21 Championship began in 1964 in response to a Congress motion put forward by the Kerry County Board. The championships have grown in importance and profile over the years, not least because the demands of the modern game mean talented players are being fielded very early in their careers, therefore the under-21s are an accurate barometer of the future fortunes of the new players and their counties.

Cork and Kerry are the most successful counties in the history of the under-21 football championship with nine titles apiece. Cork's three-in-a-row from 1984 to 1986 remains a record in the competition. One particularly notable achievement was Antrim's 1-8 to 0-10 victory over Roscommon in 1969, which gave the county its first, and to date only, All-Ireland football title. Dublin have been remarkably unsuccessful in this grade and for some years did not even field a team. Their barren spell finally ended in 2003.

The first team to win an under-21 hurling title, the Tipperary side of 1964, amassed an incredible total of forty goals and thirty-nine points in four games. Since then, Cork have stolen the show, being the most successful in under-21 hurling with eleven titles, including a four-in-a-row from 1968 to 1971. The Corkonians also did the hurling and football under-21 double in 1970 and 1971, winning both titles in the same year. The most notable feat of recent times at this level was the Limerick three-in-a-row between 2000 and 2002.

4. FAMOUS GROUNDS

Croke Park, Dublin

The Jones's Road ground, which would eventually become

Croke Park, hosted its first All-Ireland finals on 15 March 1896, when Tipperary beat Kilkenny by 6-8 to 1-0 in the hurling decider and made it a double when their footballers beat Meath by 0-4 to 0-3. Earlier finals had been played at Clonskeagh, Inchicore, Clonturk and at the Phoenix Park, other finals would take place in Cork, Thurles, Athy and Tipperary, until the GAA eventually fixed on the Dublin ground as the permanent finals venue. Accordingly, on 18 December 1913 the organisation took the step of purchasing the ground, for £1,500, from Frank Dineen, a Waterford man who would later become President of the Association. (Dineen had bought the land in 1908 from the City and Suburban Racecourse and Amusement Grounds Limited.) The newly acquired venue was named in honour of the GAA's original patron, Dr Thomas Croke, Archbishop of Cashel.

The GAA quickly made the ground their own. In 1917 the famous terrace at the Railway End of the grounds, Hill 16, was constructed, largely from the rubble left behind after the depredations of the previous year's Easter Rising. In 1924 the Hogan Stand was erected, and fourteen years later the Cusack Stand was opened to spectators. The Canal End terrace arrived in 1949, and the Nally Stand was constructed three years after that.

Croke Park has been improved regularly over the years. In 1959 the Hogan Stand was converted into a two-tier structure with seating for 16,000 people, and in 1989 Hill 16 was redeveloped. However, the last decade has seen the greatest changes in the history of the Park. The old Cusack Stand was demolished and replaced by an ultra-modern new stand, which extended to cover the old Canal End terrace. The new stand is 180 metres long, 35 metres high, seats 25,000 people and contains forty-six hospitality suites. The stadium now has a capacity of 79,500 and ranks as one of the finest in Europe, a proud symbol of the ongoing popularity and success of the GAA and Gaelic sports.

Semple Stadium, Limerick

While Croke Park is the headquarters of the GAA, Thurles' Semple Stadium is widely regarded as the spiritual home of hurling. The ground was bought by the GAA in 1910 and hosted its first Munster final four years later. It was known as the Thurles Sportsfield until a major redevelopment programme was initiated, which saw the ground reopen in 1968 as Semple Stadium. It was named after Tom Semple, a former Tipperary great and a Thurles native. One of the greatest moments in the history of Semple Stadium came in 1984 when it hosted the Centenary All-Ireland hurling final between Cork and Offaly; it has long been synonymous with memorable Munster hurling finals. The ground's capacity is almost 60,000, and it is renowned for the excellence of its surface.

Páirc Uí Chaoimh, Cork

Sometimes derided as ugly, and certainly not high on anyone's list of beloved GAA grounds, Páirc Uí Chaoimh is nevertheless one of the Association's major venues. It stands on the site of the famous Cork Athletic Grounds, which opened on 11 September 1904 with the delayed 1902 All-Ireland finals. Fittingly enough, Cork won the hurling final against London, with Dublin defeating the same opposition in the football decider. By the start of the 1970s the Athletic Grounds were showing their age and a major redevelopment programme was instigated. The new stadium, named after Pádraig Ó Caoimh, one of the GAA's greatest administrators, was opened on 6 June 1976. It has a capacity of nearly 50,000.

St Tiernach's Park, Monaghan

St Tiernach's Park in Clones was bought by the local GAA club for £700 in 1944, and opened on 6 August of that year. One of the great experiences in GAA was to watch an Ulster football final from the huge grass bank at one side of the park. The grass bank turned the venue into a natural amphitheatre, and there was simply no better place to watch a game when the weather was good. Unfortunately, it was something of a disaster when the rain poured down, so in the mid-1990s the old bank was replaced with proper seating and a new stand was constructed on the opposite side of the ground. Despite this change to the Tiernach's tradition, Clones still retains a fine atmosphere on big match days.

Fitzgerald Stadium, Killarney

Fitzgerald Stadium can lay claim to being the most beautifully situated sports ground in Ireland, nestled as it is in the shadow of the majestic Kerry Mountains. It also has the considerable added advantage of being just a short walk from the town centre, which lends Munster finals at that venue a unique party atmosphere as the crowds make the most of Killarney's plentiful bar facilities.

The ground was named after the great Kerry footballer, Dick Fitzgerald, and it opened on 31 May 1936 with a game between The Kingdom and Mayo. Though most frequently associated with Munster football finals, Killarney also has a considerable history as a hurling ground. The 1937 All-Ireland hurling final between Tipperary and Kilkenny took place there because Croke Park was closed due to the construction of the Cusack Stand. It has also hosted two of the most famous (or infamous, depending on your viewpoint) Munster hurling finals: the 1950 game when Cork fans lost the run of themselves and attacked Tipperary goalkeeper Tony Reddan, who had to be smuggled out of the ground in disguise; and the 1987 final when Tipperary beat Cork after an arid sixteen-year run without a Munster title. The stadium echoes with some of the finest memories in GAA history.

5. GAELIC FOOTBALL

Gaelic football is played by teams of fifteen-a-side, with a ball similar in size to a soccer ball. A ball kicked under the crossbar, between the posts, earns a goal, which is worth three points. A point is scored when the ball is kicked over the crossbar and between the posts. The teams include a goal-keeper, three full-backs, three half-backs, two midfielders, three half-forwards and three full-forwards who line out from right to left. The midfielders are often the dominant players in football as their ability to field high balls is perhaps the most prized skill in the game. The full-backs seldom stray more than forty yards from their side's goal, while the full-forwards are the main scorers and operate in and around the opposition goal. Half-backs and half-forwards play a more fluid type of game, moving between defence and attack as the situation demands. Goals are relatively rare in football and the ability to kick points from long range is vital for success in the game. Marking is tight, with each defender being assigned a specific man to follow. The success of attacks depends on the players' ability to undo this marking system through intricate combination play. A player is limited to four steps with the ball before he has to pass, shoot or begin another four steps by hopping the ball on the ground or on his foot (the 'solo run'), and this gives defenders a chance to dispossess him, although there is no official tackle in either Gaelic football or hurling.

The Rules of Football

If modern fans were whisked back 120 years to witness the first hurling and football matches played under the aegis of the GAA, they would notice some significant differences from the games they watch today.

An 1884 game of football, for example, would begin with the two teams lined up opposite each other in the centre of the field, holding hands, as was stipulated in the rule book. There would be twenty-one players on each team, and when the ball went out over the sideline play would be restarted by a throw-in rather than by a kick. There was no such thing as points, and no 45s, that is, a kick awarded to a team when the opposition knock the ball over their own endline. There have also been changes in the number of players on a team. In 1892 it was reduced from twenty-one to seventeen, and in 1913 it was further diminished to the fifteen which remains the case today.

A recent change has seen the number of substitutes permitted increased to five, whereas the limit was three for many years. Goalkeepers in the modern era also have considerably more protection from opposition challenges than was initially the case. They are allowed to touch the ball on the ground while in their protected fourteen-yard area, known as the Small Square. Otherwise, no player is allowed to touch the ball with his hand when the ball is on the ground.

Until 1970 hurling and football games lasted an hour. In 1970 this was changed to eighty minutes for championship matches, but this experiment was abandoned in 1975 when the duration was reduced to seventy minutes. In recent years the duration of National League matches, which previously lasted an hour, has moved up to seventy minutes. Club matches remain fixed at an hour, although they usually last a bit longer because injury time is added on. Drawn championship games are replayed on a different day, and if the replay is a draw too, extra time is played until there is a winner. There is no equivalent to soccer's penalty shoot-out, so theoretically an infinite number of replays is possible.

Surprisingly, the point as we know it did not become a part of football, or hurling, until as late as 1910. From 1886 to 1909 the goal set-up was a bit different: seven yards either side of the goalposts was a stand-alone post. When the ball was shot through the gap between one of those posts and the main goalposts, that secured one point; something similar obtains in Compromise Rules, the game played between Irish Gaelic footballers and Rules players from Australia, where one point is awarded for a 'behind' scored in this manner.

The point was something of a second-class citizen in the

early days of the GAA, and until 1892 a goal was worth more than any number of points (Had this continued, we would now be fondly remembering the famous All-Ireland victories of Galway footballers in 2000, Mayo footballers in 1997 and Offaly hurlers in 1995.) A goal was worth five points from 1892 to 1895, at which time the rules changed and it became the equivalent of three points, a situation which has remained to this day.

No playing rule has been the subject of more debate than football's handpass – striking the ball with the open hand to pass it to a fellow player – which was banned in football in 1945, but brought back the following year at the instigation of Fermanagh County Board. Four years later the handpass was again abolished, ironically after a motion proposed to Congress by Antrim, who were famous exponents of the technique. The handpass returned in 1975 and was mastered by the great Kerry and Dublin teams of the era. Six years later, probably in an attempt to somehow halt the predictable dominance of Kerry, there were moves to ban it once more. Although these efforts did not succeed, referees did clamp down on the handpass and ensure that the ball was clearly struck by one hand only. Up until then, the ball was sometimes pushed in a manner which made the handpass as close to a basketball throw as made no difference – the main reason many lovers of the game wanted it banned. In 1981, in deference to the nation's goalkeepers – who had spent the previous six years flailing helplessly as the ball was flicked over their heads by forwards – scoring by means of a handpass or with a fist from the hand was banned. This remains the position at present. (Hurling has never encountered the same trouble with the handpass as the nature of the *sliotar* means that the tactic is of limited efficacy.)

Main Rules Of Gaelic Football, 2004

1. The field of play shall be rectangular and its dimensions shall be as follows: Length: 130 metres minimum and 145

metres maximum. Width: 80 metres minimum and 90 metres maximum. The dimensions may be reduced by local bye-laws for under-15 or younger grades.

2. The scoring space shall be at the centre of each endline. Each shall be formed by two goalposts, circular in cross-section, which shall have a height of not less than 7 metres above ground level and be 6.5 metres apart. Goal nets shall be securely fixed to the back of the crossbar and the back of each goalpost.

3. A team shall consist of 15 players but a county committee may reduce the number for non-championship games. A team may start with 13 players but shall have fielded 15, inclusive of players ordered off or retired injured, by the start of the second half.

4. The football shall weigh not less than 370g and not more than 425g and have a circumference of not less than 69cms and not more than 74cms.

5. A goal shall be awarded when the ball is played over the goal-line and between the posts and under the crossbar by either team. A point is awarded when the ball is played over the crossbar between the posts by either team. A goal is equivalent to three points.

6. When a player is in possession of the ball, it may be (a) carried a maximum of four consecutive steps or held in the hand for no longer than the time needed to take four steps; (b) played from the foot to the hand – toe-tapped; (c) bounced once after each toe-tap; (d) struck with the open hand or fist, provided there is a definite striking action; (e) tossed for a kick, a toe-tap or a pass with the hand. The ball may be knocked from an opponent's hand by flicking it with the open hand.

7. Players may tackle an opponent for the ball. Provided he has at least one foot on the ground, a player may make a side-to-side charge on an opponent. When within the small rectangle, the goalkeeper may not be charged but may be

challenged for possession of the ball and the kick or pass away may be blocked. Incidental contact with the goalkeeper while playing the ball is allowed.

8. A penalty kick is awarded for an aggressive foul within the opponent's large rectangle, or for any foul within the small rectangle. The penalty kick is within the 13-metre line. A goalkeeper may move along his goal-line while a penalty kick is being taken.

9. A player who is fouled has the option of (a) taking the free kick from the hand; (b) taking the free kick from the ground; (c) allowing another player to take the free kick from the ground.

10. A score shall be allowed if, in the opinion of the referee, the ball was prevented from crossing the goal-line by anyone other than a player or a referee.

6. THE BEST FOOTBALL TEAMS

Wexford 1913–1918

The first of just three teams to win four All-Ireland football titles in a row, the great Wexford team of the pre-Independence era was also one of just two teams to reach six Leinster finals in a row (Dublin 1974–1979 was the other). After losing the 1913 and 1914 finals, Wexford won the following four football titles. The Dublin team of the 1970s and the Kildare team of 1926–1932 were the only teams to equal Wexford's record of six Leinster titles in a row.

Playing at a time when counties were represented by club teams, this famous Wexford Blue and Whites side was drawn mainly from the town of New Ross. The three central figures on the team were full-back Ned Wheeler, centre half-forward and captain Sean O'Kennedy and full-forward Aidan Doyle. Doyle, along with Dick Reynolds, Gus O'Kennedy, 'Tearin' Tom Doyle, Jim Byrne, Paddy Mackey and Tom Murphy, played in all seven of the All-Ireland finals contested by this team (the 1914 decider went to a replay). Corner-back Jim Byrne played a crucial role on the team. The finest dead-ball kicker of the day, in the 1915 final against Kerry he scored 1-2 from 50s (as 45s were known before the metric era).

Remarkably, and indeed sadly, since that golden era Wexford football has declined to such an extent that the county has not won a Leinster senior football title since 1945.

Down 1960–1961

The first team in the history of All-Ireland football to bring the Sam Maguire across the border, the Down team of the early 1960s was one of the legendary outfits of Gaelic football. The spell these fifteen men cast over the public remains unequalled: the crowds they drew for the 1960 and 1961 finals – in excess of 90,000 – remain the largest ever seen at Croke Park to this day.

Down won their first Ulster title in 1959, but were well beaten in the All-Ireland semi-final of that year by a Galway team which was in turn hammered by Kerry in the final. Yet just twelve months later the men in red and black dealt Kerry their worst ever defeat in an All-Ireland final with an ego-bruising scoreline of 2-10 to 0-8; there has been only one defeat worse for The Kingdom since: the 1972 replay against Offaly, which they lost by 1-19 to 0-13. It was an upset of seismic proportions, and when they beat Kerry again in the following year's semi-final en route to a second championship win, there were no doubts that this was a very special team indeed.

A mystique surrounded this Down team, perhaps because they seemed to have come from nowhere to filch the greatest prize. Their success owed much to the planning of Maurice Hayes, secretary of their County Board, and his fervent belief that Down were capable of making the breakthrough where other teams from across the border had failed. Alongside belief they had rigorous training courtesy of great Meath forward Peter McDermott, and were renowned for being the most physically prepared side ever seen.

The stars of the team were the half-forward trio of Sean O'Neill, Paddy Doherty and Jim McCartan. Doherty had been a professional soccer player with Lincoln City in England before returning home, serving out his ban for participation in 'foreign games', and going on to become the team's most accurate marksman. McCartan was Footballer of the Year in 1960 and 1961, while O'Neill was simply one of the greatest footballers ever to play the game. The Newry Shamrocks man starred in 1968 when another Down team beat Kerry in the final and scored one of the most extraordinary goals ever witnessed at Croke Park, but that's another story.

What made this Down side's victories extra special was that they came at a dark time for the Catholics of Northern Ireland, who were living firmly under the thumb of a repressive Unionist government. This probably accounted for some of the fanaticism with which the team was followed: when they won the 1960 final some ecstatic fans scaled the Croke Park goalposts and placed a red-and-black flag at the tip of the posts. Returning home with the victory spoils in 1960, they were stopped at the border by customs men. Unwilling to delay the longed-for moment, captain Kevin Mussen brought the Sam Maguire off the bus and the team walked across the border with the Cup as their fans celebrated. It was a hugely resonant moment.

Galway 1964–1966

This Galway three-in-a-row team was unquestionably the finest side to come out of Connacht. In three All-Ireland finals they didn't concede one goal, and in 1964 and 1966 they never looked in any danger of defeat.

Like the great Down team, Galway first had to taste disappointment in Croke Park, losing the 1963 All-Ireland final to Dublin. After that, there was no stopping them. Goalkeeper Johnny Geraghty was the best in the business, while corner-back Enda Colleran, from the small Moylough club, had no peers. Full-back Noel Tierney, from Milltown on the Mayo border, was one of the best number threes ever. The rugged John Donnellan from Dunmore and the athletic Martin Newell in the wing-back berths added to the excellence of a great defensive unit. They could also rely on an excellent half-forward line, with the free-scoring Cyril Dunne and the exciting Seamus Leydon flanking veteran centre half-forward Mattie McDonagh, the *éminence grise* who made the whole attack tick.

Galway's 1964 victory was marred by the death of former county captain Mick Donnellan, who suffered a heart attack in the stands while watching his son John captaining the team that day; John would go on to emulate his father by becoming a member of the Irish Parliament. Another son, Pat Donnellan, played a key role in the 1965 and 1966 finals, performing brilliantly at midfield despite conventional wisdom declaring that he was too small to play in that position. John's son, Michael, has kept the family tradition alive, winning All-Irelands with Galway in 1998 and 2001.

Dublin 1974–1978

It may not have been the greatest football team of all time, though it was undeniably great, but the Dublin team of the 1970s could lay claim to being the most glamorous side ever to play the game. They oozed charisma, drew huge crowds wherever they played and kick-started a GAA revival in a city where the games had been moribund for some time.

Coach Kevin Heffernan took over a county that was in the doldrums and began the journey that would take them to a record-equalling six successive All-Ireland final appearances and six Leinster titles in a row. In the process, their fans added an immense amount of colour and life to the grey, recession-hit world of 1970s Ireland.

Between 1975 and 1978 Dublin reached not only four All-Ireland finals but also all four National League finals. Had an incredible Kerry team not arisen at the same time, Dublin could well have won six in a row as the 'Big Two' were streets ahead of the competition, employing the handpass with bewildering speed and sophistication.

Dublin's 5-12 to 3-6 win against Armagh in the 1977 All-Ireland final remains a record score, as was the 2-6 scored that day by Jimmy Keaveney. Keaveney, who had retired from inter-county football and was persuaded onto the field by Heffernan, was an outstanding full-forward with a range of skills that rendered his rather portly frame irrelevant. But he was just one of the great individuals on that electrifying Dublin team. Paddy Cullen was the finest goalkeeper of his day and also a talismanic figure to the fans on Hill 16. Robbie Kelleher was an exceptional corner-back, while Kevin Moran brought the position of centre half-back to a new height of excellence before departing for a soccer career with Manchester United. Brian Mullins was a *bête noire* for opposition fans and the best midfielder of the 1970s on his day, which was often. And in addition to Keaveney, the attack included Anton 'The Blue Panther' O'Toole and Tony Hanahoe, the cunning centre half-forward who took over as team manager from Heffernan in 1977.

The team's total of three All-Irelands does not fully reflect the impact they had on Gaelic football, an impact surpassed only by the side which succeeded them at the top: Kerry.

Kerry 1975–1986

No greater team has played Gaelic football than the Kerry team managed by Mick O'Dwyer from the mid-1970s to the mid-1980s. Like the Brazilian soccer team that won the 1970 World Cup, this Kerry side was extraordinarily exciting in a way which had not been seen before and has not been seen since – and, in all likelihood, will never be seen again. They were *sui generis*, nothing less than the apotheosis of Gaelic football. On top of all that, they also lasted longer than any other great team. Over an incredible twelve-year period they won eight All-Irelands and reached two other finals. Only last-minute goals in the 1982 All-Ireland and 1983 Munster finals prevented them from putting together an incredible nine titles in a row. As it was they won a four-in-a-row, and then finished off with a three-in-a-row.

Only a county with the footballing tradition of Kerry could have produced such a team, and yet even Kerry, the home of superlative footballers, had never seen such a prodigious collection of talent. Caherciveen's Jack O'Shea at midfield was arguably the finest all-round footballer in the history of the game, and he was partnered by one of the great high-fielders in Sean Walsh. In defence, Páidí Ó Sé from the West Kerry Gaeltacht, John O'Keefe from Austin Stacks of Tralee and Tim 'The Horse' Kennelly from Listowel all rank among the all-time greats in their respective positions, while Paud Lynch and Jimmy Deenihan would have been stars on any other team.

However, it was in attack that they really shone. Mike Sheehy of Austin Stack's and Pat Spillane of Templenoe, the former stylish and composed, the latter athletic and ebullient, were two of the game's most fearsome attackers, while there have been few better full-forwards than Eoghan 'Bomber' Liston from Beale. Sneem's John Egan would have been the best attacker on most All-Ireland winning teams, but is sometimes undervalued because of the talent that surrounded him.

Everything about this unforgettable team was larger than life. They scored 9-21 in a Munster championship game, the 'Milltown Massacre', against Clare. In a National League game they beat Laois by 6-11 to no score. They won All-Ireland finals by seventeen and eleven points, won semis by twenty-two and sixteen. The goals scored by Sheehy in the 1978 final, O'Shea in 1981 and Spillane in 1986 will be replayed again and again as long as Gaelic football is played. Spillane won a record nine All-Stars, Sheehy, Ó Sé, Denis 'Ogie' Moran, Ger Power and Pat Spillane hold the record for All-Ireland winner's medals, holding eight each. Quite simply, they were the greatest.

7. FAMOUS FOOTBALL CLUBS

St Vincent's, Dublin

From the Marino area on the northside of Dublin City, St Vincent's were the inspiration behind the two finest teams ever to emerge from the capital. They provided most of the players for the team which won the 1958 All-Ireland final, Leinster titles in 1955 and 1959 and National League titles in 1953, 1955 and 1958: this was the team that proved that a side of native Dubs could compete at the top level and draw the crowds. The second team to prove that Dublin deserve a place in the history books was the outstanding side that played in the 1970s, and it too relied on St Vincent's for its star players.

In the 1950s the legendary forwards Kevin Heffernan and Ollie Freaney were the stars of both the Dublin county team and the St Vincent's club team, with dual stars Des Foley and Des 'Snitchie' Ferguson, who played hurling as well as football for the county, also making a significant contribution. Vincent's dominated Dublin football completely, winning every senior club title between 1949 and 1962. Their 1952 county final win over a star-studded Garda team drew 25,000.

In the 1970s Heffernan returned to centre stage as the manager of the greatest Dublin team of all. Once more Vincent's backboned the team, with Gay O'Driscoll, Brian Mullins, Bobby Doyle, Jimmy Keaveney and Tony Hanahoe all hailing from the club. For these club players there was also the added bonus of an All-Ireland club title in 1976 when St Vincent's beat Roscommon Gaels by seventeen points in the final.

Austin Stack's, Kerry

The amount of top-class footballers produced by the Austin Stack's club from the Rock Street area of Tralee is remarkable: twenty-eight players from the club have won a total of eighty-three All-Ireland senior medals between them. Stack's gave

Ger Power, Mike Sheehy and John O'Keefe to the great Kerry team of the 1980s and 1990s. In the 1920s and 1930s, Joe Barrett, Jackie Ryan, Miko Doyle, John Joe 'Purty' Landers and Tim 'Roundy' Landers all starred for The Kingdom and for Stack's.

The Rock Street club was founded in 1917 and became known as Austin Stack's in the 1930s; Kerryman Austin Stack was an IRA leader during the War of Independence and later a Sinn Féin TD. This area of Tralee had always been a hotbed of football and has consistently produced fine teams since the foundation of the GAA. The club has won eleven Kerry titles in total, with a highlight coming in 1977 when a win over Ballerin of Derry secured its only All-Ireland club crown.

Nemo Rangers, Cork

Nemo Rangers are the Real Madrid of club football: no other club has come near matching their record of seven All-Ireland club titles. They have also been All-Ireland runners-up three times and have won eleven Munster titles.

Based around the Capwell area on the southside of Cork City, Nemo Rangers came into existence in 1922 when the Rangers and Nemo clubs amalgamated. For many years they were notably unsuccessful and it was 1972 before they won their first Cork county title. Since then they've been unquestionably the most successful club team in the land, with All-Ireland successes in 1973, 1979, 1982, 1989, 1994 and 2002.

The driving force behind Nemo is Billy Morgan, latterly as an outstanding goalkeeper, now as an inspirational manager. Other national stars produced by the club include Frank Cogan, Colin Corkery, Joe Kavanagh, Steven O'Brien, Jimmy Kerrigan and Martin Cronin.

Crossmaglen Rangers, Armagh

A club known as the Red Hands was founded in the Crossmaglen area in 1887, but the Rangers did not come into existence until 1909. The club has won twenty-nine county titles and produced such Armagh legends as Gene Morgan, who played on the 1953 team that reached the All-Ireland final, and Joe Kernan and Tom McCreesh, who both played on the 1977 team that did the same.

Despite the quality of their players and their love of the game, for years Crossmaglen Rangers attracted attention for non-football reasons rather than for what they did on the field. Through no fault of their own they came to epitomise the prime example of the problems caused to GAA clubs by British Army activity in Northern Ireland when, from 1971 to 2001, part of the club's pitch was occupied by the security forces. The Rangers' plight became a regular rallying cry for those determined to keep Rule 21 on the GAA statute book.

In recent years, however, things have changed for the better all round, and Rangers have made the headlines for their footballing achievements, winning All-Ireland club titles in 1997, 1999 and 2000. The team was managed by Joe Kernan, the man who went on to steer Armagh to their historic All-Ireland victory in 2002. Crossmaglen men on the ground-breaking Armagh team included Oisin McConville, Francie Bellew, John McEntee and Tony McEntee.

8. FOOTBALL'S FINEST PLAYERS

There have been so many great footballers in the game that it seems invidious to pick out a few for special merit. However, it is safe to say that the men chosen here would be undisputedly regarded as truly gifted players. The teams selected by the GAA as football's and hurling's Team of the Millennium were the closest thing to a definitive list of the very best, but they were also controversial, with Jack O'Shea, for example, omitted from the football team. Like all lists of 'best ever' in sports, the question of just who were the greatest is largely subjective. But you would find very few murmurs of disapproval to the following:

Tommy Murphy (1921–1985), Laois

Tommy 'The Boy Wonder' Murphy, from Graiguecullen, is the prime example of a truly gifted player who ended his career without the ultimate honour because of the vicissitudes of geography. One of the finest footballers of all time, he never managed to win an All-Ireland medal and instead had to be content with three Leinster championship medals, in 1937, 1938 and 1946. Yet Murphy remains one of the legends of football.

He made his senior inter-county debut in 1937 at the age of sixteen while still a student in Knockbeg College. Despite his youth, Murphy was a key player on the Laois team that won the Leinster title and met Kerry in the All-Ireland semi-final. The game went to a replay and Murphy scored a brilliant goal before he was forced to retire injured thanks to some cruel treatment from the Kerry defence. The loss of Murphy unsettled Laois and they lost by a point.

In 1938 Murphy was at midfield when Laois again played Kerry in the semi-final. He gave an exhibition of high-fielding, catching the ball over his head after prodigious leaps into the air time and again, but The Kingdom still won by two points. The teenager earned the following tribute from Paddy Kennedy, another of the game's all-time greats: 'There was more football in Tommy Murphy than in any other man I came up against.'

The Boy Wonder gave a series of legendary displays in the Railway Cup during the 1940s, but his last chance of All-Ireland glory came in 1946 when, despite another superb display from their star player, Laois lost by two points to Roscommon in the All-Ireland semi-final. Murphy had scored eight points in that year's Leinster final against Kildare, but, like many great players doomed to ply their trades with counties outside the very top flight, he never got to play in an All-Ireland final. Nevertheless, he remains one of the legends of the game. In 1999, fourteen years after his death, Tommy

Murphy was selected at midfield on the Football Team of the Millennium.

Sean Purcell (1929–), Galway

Hailing from the famous Bishop Street area in the town of Tuam, County Galway, Sean Purcell may well have been the most versatile all-rounder ever to play the game of football. While Mick O'Connell (Kerry) and Jack O'Shea (Kerry) might have had a greater impact on the game, Purcell was probably the player with the greatest range. In his day he was the best in the game at the vastly different positions of full-back and centre half-forward, and he had the ability to make a major contribution in every single outfield position. He had the further advantage of being as good with his left foot as he was with his right.

Purcell's finest Croke Park hour came in the 1956 All-Ireland final when he inspired Galway to victory over Cork. Frank Stockwell, another Bishop Street man, finished with a record total score of 2-5, almost all of which was set up for him by Purcell, who was playing at centre half-forward. The uncanny understanding between the duo was such that they were known as 'the terrible twins'. But Purcell's finest display of all is considered to have been the 1954 Connacht semi-final against Mayo, when he played at full-back. In the All-Ireland semi-final of that year he was also outstanding when switched to midfield.

Renowned for his intelligence and his superlative striking of the ball, Purcell had been a colleges star with the famous St Jarlath's College of Tuam, and later steered his club, the Tuam Stars, to seven Galway titles in a row. His County Galway side won just one All-Ireland title, but they garnered five Connacht championship crowns in succession. From 1956 to 1961 Purcell averaged a remarkable seven points per championship game. He is certainly the best player to come out of Connacht in the last century, a fact reflected in his selection as centre half-forward on the Football Team of the Millennium.

Mick O'Connell (1937–), Kerry

From early in his career Mick O'Connell had a certain aura about him, a charisma, an inscrutability that made people want to talk to him but shy of doing so. Some of it had to do with the fact that he came from Valentia Island, a couple of hundred yards off the West Kerry coast: tales of O'Connell rowing solo across the waves to the mainland for matches added to the mystique. There was an aloofness which he culti-vated too, giving the impression that the adulation which is the normal lot of football legends didn't matter much to him. An apocryphal story tells of him leaving Dublin quickly after captaining Kerry to win the 1959 All-Ireland. He was safely back on Valentia by nightfall – but he had forgotten to bring the Cup with him. That was just the kind of man he was.

These are only incidental details, however. What really won O'Connell his place in the heart of football fans was the extraordinary elegance and accomplishment of his midfield play. The finest of fielders and of long-kickers, he was impos-sible to stop when in full flow. From the late 1950s to the early 1970s he set the standard by which other midfielders were judged. O'Connell was the classic exponent of catch-and-kick football, a skill that died out shortly after his inter-county retirement in 1974.

He first served notice that an exceptional talent had appeared on the scene when he totally dominated midfield and Dublin in the 1959 All-Ireland semi-final. Thirteen years later, at the age of thirty-five, he was still powerful enough to win a spot at midfield in the 1972 All-Star team. It wasn't all plain sailing for O'Connell, however. He had to endure defeats by the great Down and Galway team of the 1960s, for example, but he still ended with All-Ireland winner's medals in 1959, 1962 (when he was Footballer of the Year), 1969 and 1970. He also wrote *A Kerry Footballer*, one of the first and best GAA autobiographies, even if it doesn't really seem to fit with his reputed desire for Garboesque solitude. A popular and much-respected player, O'Connell was selected at mid-field on the Team of the Millennium.

Sean O'Neill (1940–), Down

Full-forward is *the* glamour position on a Gaelic football team – the equivalent of a striker in soccer – and there probably has never been a better number fourteen than Sean O'Neill. He certainly ranks as one of the greatest goal-scorers in the history of the game, averaging just over one goal for every three outings.

In the 1960s O'Neill was to forwards what O'Connell was to midfielders: the boss. As forward on the legendary Down team that won the 1960 and 1961 All-Irelands, the man from Newry was one-third of the greatest half-forward line in history. Though he was still an under-21, he played a crucial role in his county's historic senior victories, scoring vital goals in the 1961 semi-final against Kerry and the final against Offaly from right half-forward.

Despite that historic win, 1968 was the year of O'Neill's greatest achievement. The Down team that year was nowhere near as strong as their predecessors in the early 1960s, but the scintillating form of O'Neill at full-forward made them All-Ireland contenders. They got through to the final, where he scored one of the great Gaelic football goals of all time, managing to twist his body and stab home a shot as a high ball came back off the post towards him. Goals were O'Neill's speciality – he had scored another breathtaking one to get Down past Galway in the semi-final. In 1968 he was named Footballer of the Year, while in 1971 and 1972 he was selected on the All-Star teams (the award system only having begun in 1971).

Even in the fallow years for Down, O'Neill shone in the Railway Cup and ended his career with a record eight winner's medals in that competition. Strong, quick, intelligent, powerful in the air and elusive on the ground, he was the most feared forward of his era. On the Team of the

Above: Nicky Rackard, one of the legendary hurlers, goes through his repertoire of skills.

Above: Action from the League final in 1951, in which Meath beat Mayo 0-6 to 0-3. From left to right: Brian Smith (Meath), Jimmy Reilly (Meath), Paddy Prendergast (Mayo) and just running into the picture from the right is Peter McDermott, 'The man with the cap', also playing for Meath.

Below: Two of the greatest defenders of all time and the landscape that moulded them: Kerry greats Páidí Ó Sé and Paddy Bawn Brosnan walk along the West Kerry coast.

Above: Two of football's best fielders, Sean Walsh of Kerry and Brian Mullins of Dublin, soar high into the air in one of the many memorable contests between the counties.

Above: The great Dublin football team of the 1970s won a new and exuberant following for the GAA in the capital.

Below: First blood to Kerry in the great rivalry between the Kerry and Dublin teams of the 1970s. Ger O'Driscoll throws his arms in the air in victory after scoring the clinching goal for Kerry in the 1975 All-Ireland final – the first of five epochal championship meetings between the counties.

Above: Ger Loughnane's Clare team was both the most accomplished and the most controversial hurling side of the 1990s. Wing-forward Jamesie O'Connor, here getting a shot away under pressure, was one of Clare's stars.

Above: A goalmouth mêlée: Dublin versus Kerry in 1965. In the thick of the action, left to right, are: Seamus Murphy (Kerry), Jimmy Keaveney (Dublin), Johnny Cullity, the goalkeeper, on the ground, Mick Morris (Kerry captain), Paudie O'Donohue (Kerry), Paddy Farnan (Dublin), Niall Sheehy (Kerry) and Ger O'Connor (Kerry). The final score was Kerry 4-8, Dublin 2-6.

Left: Ladies' football enjoyed a huge upsurge in popularity in the 1990s. Here Dublin and Meath battle it out.

Above: Tipperary's team of the late 1980s and early 1990s was hugely exciting due to forwards like the brilliant Pat Fox, seen here taking on the Antrim defence in the 1989 All-Ireland hurling final.
Below: Noel Skehan, perhaps the greatest hurling goalkeeper of all time and the winner of a record seven All-Star awards in that position, is chaired off the field after Kilkenny defeated Cork in the 1983 All-Ireland hurling final.

Above: The arrival of Ulster as the dominant footballing province has been the big GAA story of modern times. The new Ulster spirit is epitomised by Kieran McGeeney of Armagh, who here contests possession with Kerry's Seamus Moynihan.

Millennium, he was chosen at right half-forward, though his finest displays arguably came at full-forward.

Jack O'Shea (1958–), Kerry

The south Kerry town of Caherciveen has produced some exceptional footballers. Jack Murphy starred for Kerry in the 1920s, as did Jerome O'Shea in the 1950s and Maurice Fitzgerald in the 1990s. The fact that Mick O'Connell's fiefdom of Valentia Island is nearby shows what an extraordinary football heartland the area is. So to class one player as the most remarkable of all south Kerry footballers is really saying something, and that honour goes to the phenomenal Jack O'Shea.

If one were to task a computer with generating a blueprint for the perfect Gaelic footballer, Jacko would have been the result. An exceptional high-fielder at midfield, he was strong enough to compete in this toughest of areas yet athletic enough to range up and down the field at top speed. No player has had such a crucial influence on so many big games.

O'Shea was as adept at shoring up Kerry's defence when it came under pressure as he was at joining the attack to make an extra man. His bullet-like drive to the net against Offaly in the 1981 All-Ireland final was one of the greatest finishes ever witnessed in Croke Park.

Kerry's five-in-a-row dreams were shattered in 1982, but O'Shea was just as authoritative from 1984 to 1986. From 1980 to 1985 he was an automatic choice at midfield on the All-Star teams, and he was named Footballer of the Year in 1980, 1981, 1984 and 1985. On the greatest team of all time, Kerry 1975–1986, he was probably the greatest player.

O'Shea was still there in the early 1990s, but he quit after Kerry's shock defeat by Clare in the 1992 Munster final. A foray into management with Mayo was not a success, but nothing can take away from the playing career of the man who might well have been the greatest footballer of all time.

9. A BRIEF HISTORY OF THE ALL-IRELAND FOOTBALL CHAMPIONSHIPS

The All-Ireland Championship is the defining competition in the GAA. All other competitions pale into insignificance compared to it and the football and hurling finals, played in September, are the most important fixtures in Irish sport.

Limerick may have been the first All-Ireland football champions, but in its early years the competition was dominated by Dublin. Between 1891 and 1902 the Dubs won eight out of twelve championships. Three of those titles were won by the Young Irelands club team who trained in the Phoenix Park and included such stars of the day as John Kennedy, Clondalkin man Darby Errity, and Dick Curtis, who was also a renowned athlete and wrestler. The Geraldines club also won three titles, while the other two were won by Kickhams, whose star player was Jack Grace, a Kilkenny man based in the capital. It must be said that the number of country footballers playing for Dublin had a lot to do with these early successes, and as migration to the capital was the norm for bright young things from other counties, this would remain so for many years.

By the turn of the century there were finals in each province, with the winners going on to contest All-Ireland semifinals. Dublin took the first All-Ireland titles, but in the 1903 final there was a harbinger of things to come when Kerry won their first title by defeating Kildare in a second replay. Kerry would go on to become the dominant force in football, and so it was fitting that they won their first title after some of the most exciting matches to date. The final was actually played in 1905 at Pat McGrath's field in Tipperary town and Kerry won by 1-4 to 1-3. But their winning goal, scored by Dick Fitzgerald – perhaps the game's first great star – was controversial and Kildare were awarded a replay after they objected. The second match was a draw as well, Kerry 0-7, Kildare 1-4, but The Kingdom came through at the third attempt by 0-8 to 0-2. Strictly speaking this was just the Home Final as Kerry still had to play London in what was termed the final proper. (London had gone straight into the final in one of the GAA's occasional sops to the emigrant population.) Kerry won that match easily.

London participated in only one other final – the 1908 decider. That final saw Dublin emulate their 1897–1899 team by completing a three-in-a-row from 1906 to 1908. Kickhams won the first two finals and Geraldines took the third. Kerry were back on top in 1909 and also won the 1913 and 1914 finals. (Cork's 1911 win over Antrim marked the first final played after the Jones's Road ground had been re-named Croke Park.) However, these finals are probably best remembered because they marked the arrival on the scene of one of the greatest football teams of all time, the Wexford Blues and Whites.

Well beaten by Kerry in their first final, Wexford lost their second in a replay. But they then became the first team to win four titles in a row, a record which has twice been equalled but will probably never be beaten. From 1915 to 1918 Wexford's footballers, in the main from New Ross, beat all comers. The 1915 final was their big breakthrough, and the crowd of 30,000 in attendance showed the extent to which Gaelic football had captured the public imagination. Goals by Aidan Doyle and Jim Byrne proved vital as Wexford held on grimly against a late Kerry rally to win 2-4 to 2-1.

The 1916 final was a much more low-key affair, played on a frosty pitch. Wexford beat Mayo 2-4 to 1-2 and made it three-in-a-row in 1917 by beating Clare 0-9 to 0-5, with legendary Wexford full-back Ned Wheeler enjoying a superb game. In 1918 the Blue and Whites were playing their sixth All-Ireland final in a row, and it wasn't surprising that this proved to be their toughest test of the whole four-in-a-row era.

The match, played on 19 February 1919, took place as the War of Independence began. The Soloheadbeg ambush, which marked the start of the conflict proper, had taken place four weeks earlier and Tipperary had been forced to train in Waterford because their county was under martial law. One of their star players, Tommy Ryan, had just been released from jail for republican activities. These disruptions didn't seem to upset Tipperary and they looked likely winners when they trailed by just one point at half-time, having played against the breeze. But history was beckoning Wexford and they summoned one last great effort to win by 0-5 to 0-4, the winning point coming from the great Gus O'Kennedy.

One interesting sidelight of this tumultuous era is that Cork owes its current famous red-and-white colours to the British Army. Up to 1918 the county had worn blue and saffron, but their strip was stolen by soldiers who raided the County Board offices. They borrowed the red-and-white jerseys of the O'Leary's Hall club, and when they won the 1919 All-Ireland while wearing them, opted to retain the lucky colours.

That the GAA managed to survive the upheavals caused by the War of Independence and the Civil War and hold All-Ireland Championships during this time was a remarkable achievement. They did not escape unscathed, however. Harassment of Association members by the Crown Forces reached a sickening height on Bloody Sunday, 21 November 1920, when British soldiers shot dead fourteen spectators and one player, Michael Hogan, at Croke Park during a football match between Tipperary and Dublin. The Civil War too left a legacy of bitterness. When Kerry reached the 1923 All-Ireland final, played in 1924, they opted initially to withdraw in protest against the continued imprisonment of GAA members who had fought on the anti-Treaty side in the Civil War. Eventually they changed their minds and though they lost the final to Dublin, a significant bridge had been crossed: football in Kerry provided a means for reconciliation between men who had fought on opposite sides in an extremely bitter conflict.

All the while there were milestones. In 1928 the Sam Maguire Cup was presented to Cavan for the first time when they beat Louth in the football final. The last football championship to run into a second year was the 1925 competition, which was eventually declared null and void because of objections, counter-objections and irregularities in the provincial championships. GAA historians generally award that lost championship to Galway, which makes it the first one won by a Connacht county.

The Dublin team which defeated the reluctant Kerry men in the 1923 final, the first decider between official county selections, was completing the county's third three-in-a-row and was one of the finest teams to come from the capital. The team was based around two clubs from the northside of the inner city, St Mary's and O'Toole's. Their finest hour came in that three-in-a-row final, which they won 1-5 to 1-3 after a classic encounter, with the two winning points coming from Joe Stynes. (Stynes was actually born in Newbridge, but the family name would become indelibly linked with Dublin GAA.)

Going for a record-equalling four in a row in the 1924 final, Dublin were upset by Kerry who won 0-4 to 0-3 with a last-gasp long-range free from Con Brosnan. Two years later Kerry were back in the final to take on Kildare in one of the most famous contests in football history. Kildare had succeeded Wexford as kings of Leinster and would equal the Blue and Whites record of six provincial titles in a row. Their star player was the remarkable centre half-forward Larry Stanley. Stanley was a top-class athlete who had won the AAA high jump title and had competed for Ireland in the same event at the Olympics. He was also one of the greatest footballers of all time. The prospect of Stanley and the glamorous Kildare side taking on Kerry attracted a record crowd of 37,500 to Croke Park.

Even by his own stratospheric standards, Stanley excelled

in that magnificent final, and with four minutes left Kildare were 0-6 to 0-3 ahead. Then Dublin's Bill Gorman managed to score an equalising goal to force a replay. Poignantly, Jack Murphy of Caherciveen, Kerry's best player in the first, drawn game, was unable to take part in the replay due to illness. (In fact, his illness proved fatal and he was buried five days after the replay.) Nonetheless, an embattled Kerry won 1-4 to 0-4, but it was a controversial victory as Stanley received rough treatment throughout. (Foul play controversies are not just a modern-day phenomenon.) Kildare did have the consolation of winning the 1927 and 1928 finals, but these victories would be overshadowed by the advent of another team for the ages: the Kerry 1929–1932 outfit, which won four All-Irelands in a row.

Kerry's golden run got underway with a win over old enemies Kildare in front of a record final crowd of 43,800, which would have been even greater had the gates not been closed before the throw-in for fear of dangerous overcrowding. Kerry squeaked home by 1-8 to 1-5, with their goal coming from newcomer Ned 'Pedlar' Sweeney. The following year's win was much easier, although it was only at the eleventh hour that Kerry decided they would play in the final, against Monaghan, following the death of the great Dick Fitzgerald. Once resolved to play, they brooked no opposition and won by 3-11 to 0-2, the second largest winning margin in a final ever. (The biggest is the nineteen points Cork had to spare over Antrim in the 1911 final, which they won by 6-6 to 1-2.)

Kerry sounded the end of an era for Kildare when they defeated the Lilywhites 1-11 to 0-8 in the 1931 final, a game notable for the appearance of Danno O'Keefe in the Kerry goals. O'Keefe would still be manning the goalmouth sixteen years later when his county played in the 1947 final and appeared in an incredible ten finals in that period. And the four in a row was completed when they beat Mayo 2-7 to 2-4 in the 1932 final. Once more, completing the four-in-a-row was difficult. A young Mayo side led by three points at half-time, but Kerry drew level thanks to a goal by Tim 'Roundy' Landers, and toughed it out in a tight finish.

Five in a row proved beyond this great team though, and they were dethroned in the 1933 semi-final by Cavan, who were beginning to build the great tradition that would see them win seventeen out of nineteen Ulster titles between 1931 and 1949. And when Cavan went on to defeat Galway 2-3 to 1-4 in the final, they became the first Ulster team to win an All-Ireland. Galway came back the next year, 1934, and by defeating Dublin by one point became the first Connacht team to win an undisputed All-Ireland. And in 1936 Mayo became the latest team to record a first-time win when they hammered fellow new kids on the block Laois by 4-11 to 0-5. Yet no matter what new forces appeared in Gaelic football, the pendulum always seemed to swing back to Kerry and they returned to their customary place at the top of the pile with one of the finest teams ever to play football.

In fact, there are those who would argue that the Kerry side of 1937–1941 was *the* best to play the game between the 1880s and the 1970s – until the might of the formidable Mick O'Dwyer Kingdom side of the 1970s and 1980s stole their mantle. Had they not lost the 1938 All-Ireland final in a replay to Galway, they would have won an unprecedented five titles in a row. As it was, they had to be content with the 1937 All-Ireland Championship and a three-in-a-row between 1939 and 1941. It was a team populated by legendary players: Danno O'Keefe in goals; Joe Keohane at full-back; Paddy Kennedy at midfield, probably among the best four or five footballers to play the game; Paddy Bawn Brosnan in the attack – though he would later become a legendary defender.

They won their first final 2-5 to 2-3 against Meath with one of their goals coming from Dan Spring, father of the former Tánaiste and Labour Party leader, Dick Spring. Revenge against Galway arrived the year after with Kennedy setting up

Charlie O'Sullivan for the last-minute point that won the game. Galway bit the dust again in 1942 by 1-8 to 0-7, with the crucial goal coming from Tom 'Gega' O'Connor, a player with a knack for getting scores at vital moments.

The next great football team came from a quarter no one would have expected. At the start of the 1940s Roscommon had not won a Connacht title in twenty-six years and were languishing in the junior competition, which catered for weaker counties. Yet by 1943 they were All-Ireland champions after one of the greatest comebacks the game has ever seen. Their star player was a flying centre half-forward called Jimmy Murray, from the village of Knockcroghery, who lifted the Sam Maguire for Roscommon after they won the 1943 final against Cavan by 2-7 to 2-2. If there had been any accusations of 'one-hit wonder', Roscommon answered them the following year by taking the title again, defeating a Kerry team with players of the calibre of Keohane, Kennedy, O'Keefe and Brosnan by 1-9 to 2-4. Roscommon might have gone on to win a third title in 1946, but Kerry held them to a draw with two late goals, and then won the replay.

The following year the champions were involved in the most incredible final of all. It wasn't the football which made the 1947 final incredible, it was the location. John 'Kerry' O'Donnell, the leading figure in New York GAA, had come up with the idea of encouraging the playing of Gaelic sports in America by hosting the final in the Big Apple. Incredibly, he and Canon Michael Hamilton, a Clare priest serving in Tipperary who represented New York on the GAA's Central Council, managed to persuade the authorities that this was more than just a pipe dream. Central Council, by a vote of 20-17, took a leap of faith and the final was fixed for the Polo Grounds, the home of the New York Giants baseball team.

The GAA's courage was rewarded. The 35,000 match tickets sold out and the final became the most fondly remembered event in Gaelic football history; among other things, it copper-fastened RTÉ commentator Micheál O'Hehir's status as the voice of the GAA. Cavan came back from an eight-point deficit to defeat Kerry 2-11 to 2-7, but the result was less important than usual. Everyone involved with the Polo Grounds final was a winner. Even if it didn't give Stateside GAA the hoped-for boost, the game had nonetheless proved that the unlikeliest moves can sometimes produce the best results. Even at this remove the idea of playing that 1947 final in New York seems unusually bold and quixotic.

The Polo Grounds victory gave an outstanding Cavan team their first of three All-Irelands. Successful again in 1948 and 1952, they were easily the most powerful side to come out of Ulster and included one of the legends of the game in centre half-back John Joe O'Reilly, who would tragically die of ill-ness at the age of just thirty-four in 1952. Aiming for a three-in-a-row in 1949, Cavan were shocked in the final by Meath, who beat them 1-10 to 1-6. Meath may have been slow to get off the mark, but henceforth they established them-selves as one of the premier footballing counties.

Mayo emulated their Roscommon neighbours with a two-in-a-row, in 1950 and 1951. Beaten by Cavan by one point in the 1948 final, they recovered and beat Louth in the 1950 decider by 2-5 to 1-6 thanks to a memorable individual goal from wing-forward Mick Flanagan. In 1951 they defeated Meath 2-8 to 0-9, with the gifted full-forward Tom Langan scoring a goal, and Sean Flanagan, later a government minis-ter, outstanding at corner-back. Incredibly, neither a Mayo nor Roscommon man has laid hands on the Sam Maguire since.

The remainder of the 1950s was a democratic time, with no county managing so much as a two-in-a-row. There were two particularly noteworthy finals, however. In 1955 a highly rated Dublin team, which had beaten All-Ireland champions Meath by twenty points in the Leinster final, came up against a Kerry team that had been more or less written off before the game even started. Dublin, with a team of home-grown players drawn largely from the St Vincent's club, had caught the imagination of the capital's sporting public and in Ollie Freaney and Kevin Heffernan had two superb forwards. But in spite of expectations – and at the expense of the punters who felt a flutter on Dublin wasn't even a gamble – Dublin lost to Kerry 0-12 to 1-6. Tadhgie Lyne scored an amazing six points for the winners.

The following year saw one of the best forward performances in football final history when Galway corner-forward Frank Stockwell scored a record 2-5 as Galway beat Cork 2-13 to 3-7. Most of Stockwell's scores were set up by his clubmate, and probably the leading footballer of the day, Sean Purcell. Stockwell's record has since been surpassed by Jimmy Keaveney, who scored 2-6 in the 1977 final, a tally equalled by Mikey Sheehy of Kerry in the 1979 final. But while Sheehy and Keaveney scored a goal from the penalty spot and points from frees, Stockwell's 2-5 all came from play. He has only been equalled in that respect by Eoghan Liston's 3-2 haul for Kerry in the 1978 final. It's difficult to see it ever being erased from the record books.

The chopping and changing at the top of the game ended when one of the most remarkable teams in the history of football came along at the start of the next decade to make an impact that perhaps only a couple of other teams have ever matched. Down came from nowhere (until 1958 they had only ever contested one Ulster final), they attracted enormous crowds (the attendances at the 1960 and 1961 finals remain the biggest ever for matches in Croke Park) and, most importantly, they were the first team to bring the Sam Maguire Cup across the border. They also played with tremendous verve and style and were tactically way ahead of their opponents. And they had players such as Sean O'Neill, Paddy Doherty and Jim McCartan, who number among the all-time greats.

Their 1960 final victory could not have been more shocking. Not only did they beat the aristocrats of football, Kerry, but they did it by a crushing 2-10 to 0-8 margin in front of 87,768 fans, with goals from McCartan and Doherty sealing Kerry's fate. The following year 90,556 people were there to see them beat Offaly 3-6 to 2-8 with a memorable McCartan goal being matched by one from O'Neill. The Down 1960–1961 team had an impact on the game which went far beyond the two All-Irelands they won, and to this day they remain the finest side from the far side of the border.

The next great team to emerge didn't have the flamboyance of Down and its strength lay in defence rather than attack. Where Down had Doherty, O'Neill and McCartan in attack, Galway had Enda Colleran, Noel Tierney and John Donnellan in defence and they built from there. In winning three finals in a row from 1964 to 1966, Galway didn't concede one goal – an incredible feat, which hasn't been matched since, and which stands as a glowing tribute to the brilliance of goalkeeper Johnny Geraghty from Kilkerrin.

What Galway had in common with Down was an ability to produce their best form in All-Ireland finals. They were regal in the 1964 0-15 to 0-10 final victory over Kerry, with top scorer Cyril Dunne bagging nine points. Things were closer the year after, but Galway got the better of Kerry again, 0-12 to 0-9, with their powerful defence holding The Kingdom to a meagre two points from play. And in 1966 the game was as good as over at half-time when Galway led by eight points against Meath. They went on to win 1-10 to 0-7, with the clinching goal coming from centre half-forward Mattie McDonagh – the only player from the 1956 side still playing. No one would have thought then that it would be thirty-one years before another Connacht team won the All-Ireland.

Galway, like Down, had proven themselves by beating Kerry – the acid test of a team's quality. Down did it again in 1968, which meant that The Kingdom had lost in three successive final appearances. But Kerry determinedly scotched any notion that this particular set of players was a bunch of losers by bouncing back to win the 1969 and 1970 finals. Despite those previous high-profile losses they were still a team to be reckoned with: from 1959 to 1970 they participated in eight out of twelve finals and won four of them.

As expected, they had the usual quota of extraordinary talents on board during this period. Johnny Cullotty had succeeded Danno O'Keefe in goals and proved to have just as much stamina, lining out in eight finals. Seamus Murphy was one of the finest ever wing-backs; Mick O'Dwyer one of the finest corner-forwards; and Mick O'Connell was just extraordinary. In hurling it's pretty much accepted that Christy Ring is the greatest player of all time, with Mick Mackey in second place. There's nothing like the same unanimity in Gaelic football, but few would dispute that O'Connell ranks in the top three at least, and had no rival as the outstanding footballer of the 1960s. Though in his thirties, he played a key role at midfield in the contrasting finals of 1969 and 1970.

The first final was a hard-fought, tense encounter in which Kerry edged past Offaly 0-10 to 0-7; while the second final, the first to be played over eighty minutes, was a free-scoring affair in which Kerry were always in control en route to a 2-19 to 0-18 win over Meath.

History was made in 1971 when Offaly became the latest county to win the Sam Maguire for the first time, with a 1-14 to 2-8 win against Galway. Offaly had trailed by five points at half-time, but inspired by swashbuckling right half-back Eugene Mulligan they bagged the title with three late scores. In 1972, in fine footballing tradition, they proved that the previous year was no fluke when they beat Kerry 1-19 to 0-13 in a replay and ended Mick O'Connell and Mick O'Dwyer's Croke Park days – on the field, at least.

In retrospect, those finals of the early 1970s pale into insignificance when compared with what came next. Within the space of just a few years GAA supporters would witness the greatest revival of all time, the greatest rivalry of all time, the greatest match of all time and the greatest team of all time, and the game itself would also change almost beyond recognition. It all began when Dublin, in the doldrums for a decade, asked Kevin Heffernan to take over their struggling football team, and he accepted.

The side Heffernan inherited was languishing in Division Two of the National League and was nobody's idea of a championship contender. Heffernan had a different idea. A combination of tactical brilliance, astute selection and, perhaps most of all, modern training methods, which ensured the players were super-fit, saw the Dubs come from nowhere to pluck the laurel wreath from the victor's brow. A Leinster quarter-final win over Offaly suggested that something was afoot in Dublin, but it was only when they defeated All-Ireland champions Cork in the All-Ireland semi-final that Heffernan's team were taken seriously. But they were still very much the outsiders as they entered the All-Ireland final against Galway. Paddy Cullen became a folk hero by saving a penalty from Liam Sammon and full-forward Jimmy Keaveney, coaxed out of retirement by Heffernan, kicked vital points as Dublin won by 0-14 to 1-6, sparking off extraordinary scenes of jubilation as the streetwise supporters of Hill 16 streamed onto the pitch, having spent the last few minutes lined up on the sidelines and behind the goals.

Heffo's Heroes were more than just a football team. They were followed with a fanaticism the GAA had not witnessed before. A fierce love of GAA, which had been lying dormant in the capital, was reawakened by their exploits as the Dubs became the team which introduced the Association to the Age of Hype. It helped too that they played immensely attractive football, although not everyone approved of their style. Dublin made the most of the reintroduction of the handpass and adopted a quick short-passing style that was anathema to cognoscenti of the traditional catch-and-kick style. The Dubs made the old style redundant and Gaelic football would never be the same again.

But football is a funny old game, as we know, and Dublin got a shock themselves in 1975 when a youthful Kerry team beat them 2-12 to 0-11 in the final. Kerry were also managed by a great forward, Mick O'Dwyer, and he had eagerly learned from Heffernan's approach. His team were also super-fit, made great use of the handpass and would eventually be recognised as the finest set of players to play the game. Dublin and Kerry were on course for a showdown.

At first it looked as though Dublin would be the team to come out on top in this fierce rivalry. They outclassed Kerry in the 1976 final, winning 3-8 to 0-10, with Kevin Moran – later to play soccer for Manchester United and the Republic of Ireland – brilliant at centre half-back. And in 1977 they seemed to have the definitive last word over Kerry when they beat them by 3-12 to 1-13 in the All-Ireland semi-final, a game widely regarded as the best ever played. The lead changed hands throughout and Kerry looked to be finishing stronger when they went two points clear with just six minutes left. Then David Hickey scored a beautiful goal for Dublin and midfielder Bernard Brogan added an even better one to clinch it for the Dubs. Their 5-12 to 3-6 cakewalk against Armagh in the final confirmed that the Big Two were playing at a completely different level from the other counties.

The pendulum swung again in the 1978 final. Dublin's dominance looked set to continue when they led by five points after twenty minutes. Then Kerry's John Egan scored a goal on the break and Mikey Sheehy added one of the most brilliant, and one of the most controversial, goals in final history. Dublin goalie Paddy Cullen was out of his goal and arguing with referee Seamus Aldridge when Sheehy curled the most delicate of shots into the net. A shattered Dublin fell apart in the second half and Eoghan 'Bomber' Liston scored three goals as Kerry won by 5-11 to 0-9 – the biggest victory margin in forty-two years. Dublin were finished as a major force, but Kerry were only getting into their stride.

In 1979 Kerry played almost perfect football. They had four all-time great attackers – Eoghan Liston, Pat Spillane, Mikey Sheehy and John Egan – marvellous defenders, such as John O'Keefe, Tim Kennelly and Paudie Lynch, and a midfielder, Jack O'Shea, who would be my personal choice for the best footballer of all time. O'Shea was an awesome athlete who seemed able to cover the whole field in a matter of seconds. He was strong, he was quick, he was an exceptional fielder and a scorer of awesome points and goals. There seemed to be nothing he and his team-mates couldn't do. No one even gave them a game in 1979, and they destroyed Dublin by 3-13 to 1-8 in the All-Ireland final.

Kerry made it three in a row in 1980, against Roscommon, toughing it out in an All-Ireland final famous for a remarkable amount of foul play, which they won by 1-9 to 1-6. They then equalled the record of the Wexford and Kerry teams of the past by making it four titles in a row in 1981. Offaly stuck with the champions for most of the game before eventually being killed off by a Jack O'Shea goal. That goal, which started at Kerry's endline and involved around half their team, seemed a perfect illustration of how accomplished this wonderful side was. They were touted as the ideal team to win a historic five-in-a-row.

It didn't happen. Holding on to a two-point lead in the closing minutes of the classic 1982 final against Offaly, Kerry conceded a spectacular goal to substitute Seamus Darby. One of the most famous goals in football history, it gave Offaly a 1-15 to 0-17 victory. Appearing rudderless and lacking in confidence, Kerry lost the 1983 Munster final and Dublin won that year's All-Ireland, beating Galway in a game mainly notable for four sendings-off and an enormous amount of bad feeling.

But, incredibly, Kerry weren't finished yet: the adage about wounded animals sums up what happened next. Their veterans, helped by a few new additions, returned to put together a wholly unexpected three-in-a-row between 1984 and 1986. They weren't the same unparalleled force they had been during their first coming, but then, who has been? Pat Spillane gave one of the great individual finals displays when they defeated Dublin 0-14 to 1-6 in the 1984 final and Dublin were again the victims in 1985. The 1986 final was a fitting send-off for this team of all the talents. They trailed by seven points to Tyrone in the second half before summoning up one last burst of brilliance which saw them romp home 2-15 to 1-10. The crucial scores were spectacular goals by Spillane and Sheehy – after O'Shea, probably the supreme talents on the team.

The departure of that Kerry team was greeted with a certain amount of relief. They had been wonderful to watch, but their dominance had become monotonous in the end. Instead of rising to the challenge posed by The Kingdom, too many counties seemed to become demoralised and lose the game before the opening whistle blew. Yet without Kerry, the championship was in danger of being a bit of an anti-climax.

Thankfully they were succeeded by two fine teams, the Meath side which won the 1987 and 1988 All-Irelands and the Cork team which won in 1989 and 1990. Both were good outfits, capable of fine attacking football, but they were often associated in the public mind with a physical approach that verged on the intimidatory. In fact, the Cork–Meath final of 1989, won 0-17 to 1-11 by Cork, was one of the best matches of the decade. However, what many fans remember are the bruising replayed final of 1988 between the teams and the grim 1990 decider. Meath and Cork seemed to bring out the worst in each other and as a result have gained unfair reputations for ruthlessness, which means so many other things get overlooked or forgotten. For example, the most notable feature of the 1990 final was that the victorious Cork team included Teddy McCarthy, who had played for the county's hurling team earlier in the month in their defeat of Galway. The Glanmire man thus became the only player in the history of the GAA to win All-Ireland senior hurling and football medals in the same year.

The period since 1990 has been notable for its unpredictability. Amazingly, no county was able to win even a second title in a row in the thirteen years between 1990 and 2003. This has never happened before in the history of the All-Ireland competition. It has also been a period of great breakthroughs with four counties – Donegal, Derry, Armagh and Tyrone – winning their first All-Irelands. It took a much longer period, from 1943 to 1971, for the previous four debut champions to come through. And it has also been a time when Connacht and Ulster have re-emerged as challengers to the traditional power provinces. Down's 1991 final win over Meath, perhaps the one which definitively heralded the new era, was the first by an Ulster county for twenty-three years, while Galway's 1998 final win over Kildare was Connacht's first victory in thirty-two years. All of this is a breath of life to the game, and increases interest in the competitions: everyone is a contender.

It has been a time when counties have achieved the unimaginable. Donegal were rank underdogs when they beat Dublin 0-18 to 0-14 in 1992, and Derry were appearing in only their second final ever when they defeated Cork 1-14 to 2-8 a year later. It was Armagh's turn to make history in 2002 when they beat Kerry by a point. A year later there was confirmation that the new era belonged to Ulster when Tyrone beat their neighbours, Armagh, 0-12 to 0-9 in the first final to be contested by two teams from the same province.

This new era has been made possible by structural changes in the championship, mainly the introduction of a 'back-door' system, which allows defeated teams another shot at the title. Defeat in the provincial championships no longer spells automatic elimination from the All-Ireland. Galway was the first team to lose a game and win the title. In 2001 they lost the Connacht semi-final to Roscommon, but battled their way through the back-door and defeated Meath in the final.

Galway are one of three teams who have vied for dominance over the past decade. Kerry – who had gone an amazing eleven years without an All-Ireland after their great team had broken up in 1986 – enjoyed a glorious comeback in 1997, beating Mayo with an astounding display from Maurice Fitzgerald, the latest off The Kingdom's conveyor belt that produces footballing geniuses. They beat Galway 0-17 to 1-10 in the replay of the 2000 final. Galway's 1-14 to 1-11 win over Kildare in 1998 was a huge shock to many people, as indeed was that win over Meath in 2001. Meath is throwing everything they have at their opponents in a bid to make their name as a force to be reckoned with. They re-emerged as a power in 1996 after a replay win over Mayo in a game marred by an enormous punch-up that distracted from a thrilling second half. Three years later they beat Cork 1-11 to 1-9 in the worst final of the decade, a dour game marked by frequent fouling and sloppy play. But, like Galway and Kerry, they couldn't manage to dominate. Perhaps the days of domination are over and we'll see even more counties breaking through in the next decade. In Laois and Westmeath, Sligo and Monaghan, they certainly hope so.

Number of All-Ireland senior football titles held by the winning counties:

33 – Kerry

22 – Dublin

9 – Galway

7 – Meath

6 – Cork

5 – Wexford, Cavan, Down

4 – Kildare, Tipperary

3 – Louth, Mayo, Offaly

2 – Limerick, Roscommon

1 – Donegal, Derry, Tyrone, Armagh

10. LADIES' FOOTBALL

Ladies' football has nothing like as long a history as camogie, the traditional Gaelic sport for women, but recently it has begun to surpass the older game in popularity and achieve an enviably high public profile.

The Ladies' Football Association was established in 1974. The founders showed an admirable sense of history by holding their inaugural meeting in Hayes's Hotel, Thurles, furthermore a Tipperary man, Jim Kennedy, was nominated as the Association's first President. The theme of Tipperary dominance continued when the county won the first ever Ladies All-Ireland title, defeating Offaly by 2-3 to 2-2 at Durrow. The six other counties that participated in the first championship were Roscommon, Laois, Galway, Kerry, Cork and Waterford.

It wasn't until 1982 that one county emerged as a dominant force. Not surprisingly, that county was Kerry. The Kingdom won an incredible nine titles in a row between 1982 and 1990, and midfielder Mary Jo Curran established herself as the finest player in the game, while full-forward Del Whyte and wing-forward Marina Barry also excelled. When Kerry were dethroned it was by a somewhat unlikely opponent. Waterford have never been a force in men's football, but the women's team from the county, backboned by the Ballymacarbery club in the west of the county, replaced Kerry at the top in 1990.

Waterford won four out of the five titles between 1991 and 1995 and, perhaps more importantly, their epic final battles with Monaghan in 1997 and 1998 catapulted the sport into public awareness. The counties won one title apiece and the standard of play displayed by Áine Wall, Geraldine O'Ryan and Annalisa Crotty for Waterford, and Jenny Greenan, Linda Farrelly and Edel Byrne for Monaghan caught the public imagination.

Restored to the top in 1998, Waterford entered the 1999 All-Ireland final as incredibly hot favourites to defeat Mayo. They lost in one of the game's greatest upsets and the young Mayo side that beat them has proven that victory was no fluke by winning the 2000, 2002 and 2003 titles. They were denied a three-in-a-row by Laois in 2001, a hugely popular victory because it finally rewarded Sue Ramsbottom, one of the game's finest players, with an All-Ireland medal.

For the moment, however, Mayo are back on top and players such as Cora Staunton, Christine Heffernan and Helena Lohan have raised the bar for ladies' football in the new millennium. It's a far cry from the early days of the Association when, as the first President admitted, male spectators largely came along for a laugh. They're not laughing now.

11. HURLING

Hurling is the fastest field game in the world and it's also unique, appearing to have little in common with any other sport. Perhaps hockey and lacrosse are its closest relatives, but they're still very distant ones. Its players use a *camán*, or hurley (similar to a hockey stick) to shunt a small ball around the pitch at speeds of up to a hundred miles per hour. The ball is made of hemp covered in leather and is called a *sliotar* (pron. Shli-ther).

The game has not changed too much, despite being centuries old, although some key differences do apply. If we send our modern fans back in time again to the matches of the GAA's early days, the games would have begun the same way, but would have been played on a pitch of gargantuan proportions: 200 yards long by 150 yards wide. They had just two umpires whereas there are now four, and when restarting the game an official would throw the ball in, as opposed to the modern game which uses the sideline cut. The sideline puck, used to restart the game when the ball has been sent over the sideline, was introduced in 1899. Instead of 65s, the attacking team would have been awarded a 20-yard free. Thankfully, the rule allowing players to wrestle an opponent to the ground bit the dust in 1886.

Ancient in origin, hurling is mentioned in legend and folk-tale and the great players are regarded as being artists as much as sportsmen. Such is the respect which hurlers command among Irish people that Jack Lynch, one of the greatest Cork players, became Taoiseach (prime minister) of the country. While football is now played far more widely, it is hurling which has, and always will have, pride of place in the affections of GAA supporters. Anyone visiting Ireland should try to see a hurling game, as it is an experience not to be missed.

Main Rules of Hurling, 2004

1. The field of play shall be rectangular and its dimensions shall be as follows: Length: 130 metres minimum and 145 metres maximum; Width: 80 metres minimum and 90 metres maximum. The dimensions may be reduced by local bye-laws for under-15 or younger grades.

2. The ball may be struck with the hurley when it is on the ground, in the air, tossed from the hand, or lifted with the hurley.

3. A player may run with the ball balanced on or hopping on his hurley. A player may catch the ball, play it on his hurley and bring it back on his hand once. A player who has not caught the ball may play it from the hurley into his hand twice. The ball may be struck with the hand, kicked or lifted off the

ground with the feet.

4. The ball may not be touched on the ground with the hand except when a player is knocked down or falls and the ball in his hand touches the ground. The ball may be carried in his hand for a maximum of four consecutive steps or held in the hand for no longer than the time needed to take four steps.

5. Players may tackle an opponent for the ball. Provided that at least one foot remains on the ground, a player may make a side-to-side charge on an opponent who is (a) in possession of the ball, or (b) who is playing the ball, or (c) when both players are running in the direction of the ball to play it.

6. For a run-up to a free puck, sideline puck or puck-out, a player may go outside the boundary lines, but otherwise players shall remain within the field of play.

7. A goal is scored when the ball is played over the goal-line between the posts and under the crossbar by either team. A point is scored when the ball is played over the crossbar between the posts by either team. A goal is equivalent to three points.

8. For all free pucks, including penalties, the ball may be struck with the hurley in either of two ways: (a) lift the ball with the hurley at the first attempt and strike it with the hurley or (b) strike the ball off the ground.

9. A penalty puck shall be awarded for an aggressive foul within the large rectangle. The penalty puck shall be taken from the centre-point of the 20-metre line. A free puck from the centre of the 20-metre line shall be awarded for a technical foul within the large rectangle. Only three players may remain on the goal-line to defend against a penalty by the opposition.

10. When a ball is played over the endline and outside the goalposts by the team defending that end, a free puck shall be awarded to the opposing team on the 65-metre line, opposite where the ball crossed the endline.

12. THE BEST HURLING TEAMS

Limerick 1934–1940

If All-Ireland titles are anything to go by, Limerick can claim to be the strongest hurling county outside the Big Three of Tipperary, Cork and Kilkenny, with a haul of seven titles. However, the last of these wins came in 1973 and the reality of Limerick's hurling pedigree is that it was home to one of the most exciting of all hurling teams in the 1930s and early 1940s.

Between 1934 and 1940, Limerick won five Munster titles, five National League titles in a row and three All-Ireland titles, and lost another two finals narrowly. Between October 1933 and April 1938 the team played sixty-five matches and lost just three of them. They were by far the best team of a highly competitive era. The team drew crowds like no one else ever had: the attendances for the 1933 and 1935 All-Ireland finals and the 1939 Munster final were all record-breaking.

Limerick were inspired by the presence in their ranks of the second greatest hurler of all time, Mick Mackey, who played his club hurling with Ahane, the club that backboned the Limerick team and won fifteen county senior titles between 1931 and 1948. At one stage Ahane supplied an unprecedented seven players to the Munster Railway Cup team.

Their reputation as the great entertainers of the game was partly due to Mackey's willingness to put the ball on the hurl and run at opposition defences. But it was not a one-man show. The great man had the advantage of being surrounded by other excellent players: Paddy Scanlan was one of the greatest goalkeepers the game has produced and he got his side out of many a tight corner; Dave Clohessy had an extraordinary record as a goal-poacher; Timmy Ryan, famous for his striking of the *sliotar* in mid-air and known as 'Golden Miller' after the great steeplechaser of the time, dominated midfield in most matches; and speedster Jackie Power was one of the most feared forwards of his day. Together these men played hurling as a form of poetry – graceful, athletic, skilful and hard-hitting.

Cork 1941–1944

By one important yardstick this Cork team of the 1940s was the finest of all hurling teams: they remain the only side to have won four All-Ireland titles in a row. However, they did not face the toughest of opposition in those All-Ireland finals, so the jury is still out on the question of whether they can be considered to be the greatest team ever.

They were certainly great, though. Nine players appeared in all four finals: Christy Ring, Jack Lynch, Din Joe Buckley, Jim Young, Willie 'Long Puck' Murphy, Paddy O'Donovan, Alan Lotty, Batt Thornhill and John Quirke. Five of those came from the superb Glen Rovers team in Cork City, among them Ring, the undisputed best hurler ever, and Lynch, one of the best midfielders ever. Cork also had an excellent manager in Jim 'Tough' Barry, who was in charge of the county's hurling teams over a period of forty years.

Cork's toughest contests in their four-in-a-row years came in Munster finals. In 1943 they were put to the pin of their collar before defeating Waterford by 3-13 to 3-8, with Ring's contribution of 1-3 proving vital. And in 1944 they played Limerick in what became known as the Great Bicycle Finals. Transport restrictions necessitated by the Second World War meant that fans were forced to cycle or walk to Thurles if they wanted to see the finals. Those who did were awarded with two of the finest games ever played. A hat-trick of goals from Johnny Quirke earned Cork a draw, 6-7, against Limerick, 4-13, in the first match. In the replay Cork trailed by four points with just seven minutes left, but equalised thanks to a Jim Morrison goal and a Quirke point. Then a last-gasp goal from Ring gave them a 4-6 to 3-6 victory. Cork also had a tough semi-final match that year, beating Galway by just one point.

Cork's teams of the time were full of quality players. There was Mick Kennefick, the defender who was viewed as potentially an even greater talent than Ring and won his first All-Ireland medal at the age of eighteen before being forced to retire through injury just a year later. Half-forward Sean Condon was another prodigy whose career was cut short through injury, while Joe Kelly, the Irish sprint champion, made a spectacular impact at corner-forward before emigrating to New Zealand at the height of his fame. That four-in-a-row record may never be beaten.

In addition to possessing a host of quality players, Cork were fortunate in having a settled team with experienced hurlers who had played plenty of championship games. Allied to the shrewd management of Christy Ring and the cohesion lent to the team by its central core of Glen Rovers players, this made them unbeatable on their day.

Wexford 1951–1956

The Wexford hurling team of the 1950s was similar in some ways to the Down football team of the 1960s. The side brought their county out of the doldrums and back into the major league: their 1951 All-Ireland final appearance was the county's first in thirty-three years, their 1955 All-Ireland final victory the first in forty-five; it contained some of the game's most charismatic figures; and it was hugely popular – the 1954 and 1956 hurling finals drew the sport's biggest ever crowds, a record which stands to this day. And like that Down team, Wexford won only two All-Irelands but their true impact was far greater.

Despite this litany of outstanding achievement, there had been a time when the team looked set to under-achieve. After making it to the 1951 All-Ireland they suffered shocking losses in the next two Leinster deciders, and after the 1954 final there was a feeling that the team's big chance had been lost. Thankfully, that wasn't to be the case because there was something larger-than-life about this team. They were as renowned for their sportsmanship as for their talent, and the game would have been the poorer had they gone unrewarded.

The team will always be associated with the three Rackards from Rathnure. Nicky, probably the greatest of all full-forwards, the majestic cap-wearing Bobbie and the relatively unsung Billy. They had perhaps the game's finest full-back, Nick O'Donnell, plus the perfect foils for Nicky Rackard in the shape of the speedy Tim Flood and Padge Kehoe.

Perhaps their most remarkable victory came in the 1956 National League final when they trailed by fifteen points to Tipperary at half-time, but came back and won the match by eight points. When on form, they had a penchant for the spectacular that no one could match.

Tipperary 1961–1965

The Tipperary team of the 1960s remains firmly associated in the public mind with 'Hell's Kitchen', the appropriately named full-back line that was probably the most physically fearsome unit ever to play the game. Cork's Justin McCarthy, who played against them, reckoned that 70% of the team's game consisted of physically intimidating the opposition.

However, to focus solely on the physical toughness that underpinned their game would be to do an injustice to the greatest Tipperary side of all. They were also a cerebral team; centre half-back Tony Wall wrote the first indepth study of hurling. Plus, they had technique and style in spades. With a forward line that included Donie Nealon, Sean McLoughlin, Liam Devaney and the great Jimmy Doyle, flair players one and all, Tipp didn't need to rely on brute force. Midfielders Theo English and Mick Roche were considerable stylists too and when Tipperary took flight, no one could ground them.

Tipperary was undoubtedly the leading county in hurling during the 1960s. In addition to the four titles won by the 1961–1965 team they reached the finals in 1960, 1967 and 1968, losing twice to Wexford and once to Kilkenny. For Tipp natives, the true measure of their golden era is taken in relation to Cork, the rivals who matter most to Tipp hurlers and fans: between 1958 and 1968 Cork did not have one win against Tipperary. It may not be the most fondly remembered team in hurling history, but the 'Hell's Kitchen' side was undoubtedly one of the finest.

Kilkenny 1971–1975

The legendary Munster Championship matches between Cork and Tipperary from 1949 to 1954 were responsible for the widely held notion that hurling in the province was far ahead of that in Leinster, and that Cork, Tipp and Limerick were the creams of the Munster crop. Accordingly, Kilkenny was seen as the junior partner of the Big Three for the next few decades. That perception took a battering after two landmark victories. Their defeat of Tipperary in the 1967 final was Kilkenny's first All-Ireland win over Tipp in forty-five years; their win over Cork in 1969 was their first over the Rebels in twenty-two years. The ranking had changed for good.

Since then, Kilkenny can claim to be the dominant force in hurling. From the 1970s on their tally of All-Irelands (11) far outstrips that of Cork (8) and Tipperary (4). Fine teams from the county have completed a remarkable sequence of two-in-a-rows, winning the Liam McCarthy Cup in 1982 and 1983, 1992 and 1993 and 2002 and 2003. (Had it not been for an injury crisis, they could well have done the same in 1972 and 1973. Get your bets on now for 2012 and 2013!)

The best of all those Kilkenny teams was the one which contested five All-Ireland finals in a row, winning three of them. The aforementioned injury crisis probably denied them a record-equalling four-in-a-row. Their star player was Eddie Keher, a sharp-shooting wing-forward from the 1960s who had moved into the left corner in the final years of his career and seemed to be getting better with age. They also had a contender for the finest goalkeeper of all time in Noel Skehan, who had understudied the great Ollie Walsh for years before making the most of his chance to prove his worth in the Kilkenny net.

Skehan got plenty of practice because this Kilkenny team played an open style of hurling that meant their matches were characterised by a huge number of shots at goal – by both sides. They were involved in some thrilling high-scoring shootouts: 3-24 to 5-11 against Cork in the 1972 All-Ireland final; a 5-14 to 5-17 loss to Tipperary in the 1971 final; a 6-13 draw with Wexford in the 1972 Leinster final; and a 6-13 to 2-24 win over Wexford in the 1974 provincial decider. Needless to say, this made the Cats exceptionally entertaining for spectators.

In addition to Keher and Skehan, tough corner-back Fan Larkin, commanding centre half-back Pat Henderson, midfielders Frank Cummins and Liam 'Chunky' O'Brien and centre half-forward Pat Delaney will feature on any list of great players. When Kilkenny won the 1993 All-Ireland final against Cork, PJ Delaney, Pat's son, was their outstanding player. Philly Larkin, Fan's son, was just as good when they beat Clare in the 2002 final. The seam of gold is far from exhausted in black-and-amber country.

13. FAMOUS HURLING CLUBS

Blackrock, Cork
In a city that boasts three of the game's greatest clubs, Blackrock, on the southside of the city, may be the best of them all. The club has been a member of the hurling aristocracy since it was founded in 1883, a year before the GAA itself got going. Blackrock won eight of the first nine Cork titles and, this being in the days when clubs represented counties, added the All-Irelands of 1893 and 1894 for good measure. They went on to win the 1903 All-Ireland and were such a dominant force in Cork hurling that up until the early 1930s the Blackrock club selected the county team.

Over the years their hegemony was challenged by Glen

Rovers and St Finbarr's, but Blackrock have always been close to the top. They enjoyed a golden spell in the 1970s with All-Ireland club titles in 1972, 1974 and 1979, along with five Munster titles in that same decade. That wonderful 1970s team included inter-county stars such as John Horgan, Pat Moylan, Ray Cummins, Dermot McCurtain and Tom Cashman, who all played key roles for the Cork three-in-a-row team.

The tradition of Blackrock men contributing to great Cork teams has been pretty much a constant. The star players on the famous 1931 Cork team – Eudie Coughlan, Paddy 'Balty' Aherne and Mick 'Gah' Ahearne – all hailed from Blackrock, which supplied the majority of players on the side. Over sixty years later, when Cork won the 1999 All-Ireland against Kilkenny, it was the Blackrock trio of Wayne Sherlock, John Browne and Fergal Ryan who were outstanding in defence. Blackrock is a tradition that looks set to continue, and Cork can be grateful for that.

Glen Rovers, Cork

In the 1930s Glen Rovers, from the Glen and Blackpool areas on the northside of Cork City, took over from Blackrock as kings of Cork hurling. From 1932 to 1941 they won ten county titles in a row, a remarkable feat given the level of competitiveness in club hurling in Cork. It was arguably the finest club team ever, and had there been an All-Ireland club championship back then (the competition began in 1971), the Glen would undoubtedly have scooped several titles.

Five Glen players were ever-presents on the Cork team that won a record four All-Ireland titles in a row from 1941 to 1944, they were: Jack Lynch, Din Joe Buckley, Jim Young, Paddy O'Donovan and Christy Ring (who had joined the club from Cloyne). Another Glen man to shine in the county jersey was Dave Creedon, goalkeeper on the 1952–1954 Cork team, who conceded just one goal in three All-Ireland finals. His clubmate, Josie Hartnett, also excelled at centre half-forward.

The Glen contributed to the golden age of Cork club

hurling in the 1970s. They provided the unparalleled defenders Denis Coughlan and Martin O'Doherty to the county team, and also won All-Ireland titles in 1973 and 1977. The Glen's tradition of skilful forward play continued in the 1980s and 1990s with outstanding centre half-forward Tomás Mulcahy carving out a national reputation, though they have fallen behind their old rivals, Blackrock, at club level.

Ballyhale Shamrocks, Kilkenny

The success enjoyed by the small Ballyhale club from south Kilkenny is testimony to the influence one family can have on a GAA team. When the Shamrocks won the All-Ireland club hurling titles in 1981, 1984 and 1990 there were no less than seven Fennelly brothers on the team.

The magnificent septet were Michael, Ger, Kevin, Brendan, Liam, Sean and Dermot. All of them represented Kilkenny, with Ger, Kevin, Liam and Sean figuring on the county team that lost to Galway in the 1987 All-Ireland final. Liam, the most talented of the family, was one of the finest forwards of the 1980s and 1990s and captained Kilkenny to an All-Ireland victory in 1992, emulating the feat of Ger thirteen years earlier.

Ballyhale Shamrocks was founded in 1972 with the amalgamation of two clubs in the Ballyhale parish. Kevin Fennelly Senior, the father of the seven brothers, had played a key role in the amalgamation, as had Fr Sean Reid. To continue the family theme, Fr Reid's nephew, Richie, also a Kilkenny senior player, was captain when Ballyhale won their first All-Ireland title in 1981. Their third victory, in 1990, brought Shamrocks level with the mighty Blackrock as the most successful side in the All-Ireland club hurling championships. Since then only Birr, from Offaly, has won more titles.

And although families like the Fennellys come along only once in a blue moon, the Ballyhale flag was kept flying on the national stage when the brilliant Henry Shefflin won Hurler of the Year honours in 2002.

Birr, Offaly

When Blackrock's star-studded team was dominating the club hurling scene in the 1970s, no one would have imagined that they would be superseded as the finest team of modern times by Birr.

For a start, Offaly was never a strong hurling county. Secondly, Birr wasn't even one of the strongest clubs in Offaly at the time. Nevertheless, when they beat Dunloy of Antrim in the 2003 final, Birr became the first club to win four All-Ireland club titles. Victories in 1995, 1998, 2002 and 2003 confirmed the Offaly champions as the leading club of the day.

Once again there was a strong family element to the success story. Inspirational manager Pad Joe Whelehan was one of the key characters behind the rise of Birr and his son, Brian, one of the greatest wing-backs of all time, was another. Add in the part played by Barry and Simon Whelehan and it's clear that without Pad Joe and his brood, Birr might have remained also-rans.

There were other players who distinguished themselves for Offaly and for Birr: Joe Errity, Gary Hannify and Declan and Johnny Pilkington, in particular. And when Birr won their two-in-a-row in 2002 and 2003, young players such as John Paul O'Meara and Steven Browne showed that the Birr hurling dynasty was set to carry on. Like Offaly, they were here to stay – at the top.

SPECIAL MENTION: St Finbarr's, Cork

There are great hurling clubs and there are great football clubs, but St Finbarr's enjoys the enviable distinction of being a great dual club. Located on the southside of Cork City, the Barrs are the only club to have won All-Ireland titles in both hurling and football, an immense achievement that is unlikely to be challenged for many years.

St Finbarr's was the third member of the triumvirate that dominated Cork hurling for most of its history. Given that Blackrock and Glen Rovers were winning All-Ireland club titles in the 1970s, the Barrs were hardly going to be left out. Their victorious teams in 1975 and 1978 included county players Charlie McCarthy, Gerald McCarthy, Tony Maher, Con Roche and Jimmy Barry-Murphy. Barry-Murphy, perhaps the most gifted dual player of all, was inspirational on the Barrs' football team that won All-Irelands in 1980 and 1981. So too was Christy Ryan, who had graduated to become the elder statesman of the team when they won their third All-Ireland in 1987.

14. HURLING'S FINEST PLAYERS

Mick Mackey (1912–1982), Limerick

They say that second-best is never remembered, but Mick Mackey has proven that adage wrong. He is almost unanimously reckoned to be the second-best hurler of all time: the only man who could be said to have bested him was the unique Christy Ring. But Mackey is remembered with the same adulation, respect and awe by those who witnessed this master of the game in action.

Nicknamed The Playboy of the Southern World, Mackey inspired great affection because he played with such abandon and enjoyed himself on the pitch. As his team-mate Jackie O'Connell put it, hurling was just one part of Mackey's life – a passion, yes, but not the whole of the man. In Mackey's own words: 'I was a cool class of a customer. It was good crack. Maybe Ring didn't get the same fun out of it.' The ESB van driver from Castleconnell played with a smile on his face and seemed to embark on his famous solo runs just for the joy it gave to the spectators. In modern parlance, he didn't have any hang-ups about his performance, he just played.

He was extraordinarily powerful, standing over six feet tall and weighing a well-muscled thirteen stone; many opponents were in awe of his physical appearance – a very good card for a hurler to hold. Christy Ring loved to tell a story of how a

Cork player punched Mackey, 'and Mackey went twice round the pitch after him and the only thing that stopped [the Cork player] running home to Cork was the palings around the ground.'

Mackey's presence on the pitch was enough to draw several thousand extra spectators to big games. He was one of the country's great popular entertainers – a sporting equivalent of the silver-screen heroes played by the likes of Errol Flynn and Tyrone Power. Neither Limerick nor any other county has seen his like since: he was a one-off, and they smashed the mould to pieces after him.

Christy Ring (1920–1979), Cork

Ring was hurling's Shakespeare, its Pelé, its Mozart. He came as close to perfection as any sportsman can. Sometimes it's difficult to think of Christy Ring as a hurler who took to the field Sunday after Sunday with twenty-nine other players. The words 'Christy Ring' seem more connected to legend than to the reality of the pitch, as if he were a figure from some heroic tale of yore whose impossible deeds exist only in the storyteller's mind. He seemed an anachronism – a reincarnation of Cúchulainn for the modern age. But Christy Ring was real all right.

Ring grew up in the East Cork village of Cloyne and spent his evenings tirelessly pucking a *sliotar* around in the back garden, near the pitch which is now fronted by a statue of him. He became a player who moved like a dancer, was as strong as a bull, quick as a top-class sprinter and wielded the *camán* like a sorcerer. The statistics are quite simply staggering: he scored three goals in four minutes in the 1956 Munster final; he beat five Kilkenny players to score the greatest All-Ireland final goal in 1946; and in the 1953 Munster final he scored an equalising point and was quickly back on his goal-line to stop a 21-yard free. In almost every game he did something that the crowd would talk about for weeks afterwards.

Ring's extraordinary life was cut short in 1979 when, at the age of fifty-eight, he suffered a heart attack in Cork City. A giant had fallen. Jack Lynch, an old team-mate, was so upset that some observers believe it contributed to the Taoiseach's resignation from office soon thereafter. Christy Ring made an impact, in life and in death, like no Irish sportsman ever has or ever will again. He won eight All-Ireland medals, nine Munster medals and fourteen Cork championships with Glen Rovers, the city club he joined in 1941 after a falling-out with Cloyne. Ring became one of their own in the Glen. A genius belongs to everybody.

John Doyle (1930–), Tipperary

The first defender to become a big star, John Doyle was undoubtedly the finest corner-back ever seen, but his name was also a by-word for a toughness that teetered on the edge of legality. In a Western movie, John Doyle would have been played by Robert Ryan, wearing a black hat.

His bruising physicality aside, it would be foolish to down-play Doyle's hurling ability. Over six feet tall and weighing thirteen-and-a-half stone at his peak, the man from the Holy-cross club was deceptively quick over short distances and his often-underestimated skill enabled him to make clearances in the tightest of situations. When he decided to burst through a pack of attackers, there was no stopping him. And while he might have dished out the punishment, he could take it too. His was the uncomplicated creed of the genuine hard man: 'We lived in a tougher and harder school,' he once said.

Doyle won eight All-Ireland medals, picking them up in three different decades. He first caught the eye as a young corner-back on the 1949–1951 Tipperary team, but will for-ever be associated with Hell's Kitchen, the ruthless full-back line he made up along with Michael Maher and Kieran Carey on the legendary Tipp team of the 1960s. In his own way, John Doyle is as much of a legend as Mackey or Ring. After all, great drama needs both heroes and villains.

Nicky Rackard (1922–1975), Wexford

There has never been a scoring machine like Nicky Rackard; the Rathnure man could compile totals which seemed to defy logic. In the 1954 championship, for example, he scored 5-4 in the Leinster final against Dublin and a record 7-7 in the All-Ireland semi-final against Antrim. In 1956 he scored 5-3 in the All-Ireland semi-final against Galway and finished the season with thirty-five goals and fifty points. In the 1952 League final against Tipperary he scored a hat-trick of goals from 21-yard frees. So unstoppable was he from that position that when the Westmeath goalkeeper stopped one of Rackard's attempts at goal from a 21-yard free in the 1955 Leinster semi-final, he received a standing ovation from the crowd.

The big full-forward was joined on Wexford's All-Ireland winning teams in 1955 and 1956 by his brothers Bobbie and Billie (another brother, Jimmy, played on the losing All-Ireland final team of 1951). From his days in the famous hurling nursery of St Kieran's College, Kilkenny, Rackard had been regarded as a star in the making, but he began his inter-county career when Wexford were in the doldrums, apparently doomed to forever play second fiddle to Kilkenny. But true sporting genius is as much mental as it is physical, and Nicky Rackard, above anyone else, inspired the great Wexford hurling revival. It was fitting then that it was he who scored the clinching goal in the 1956 final victory over Cork that confirmed the greatness of his team.

He retired after that historic game and soon faced the toughest opponent of his life: alcoholism. After years of struggle and anguish, Rackard finally gave up alcohol and began to help other alcoholics recover from the disease. By the time of his death in 1975, at the age of fifty-three, he had proven to be an even greater hero off the pitch than he had been on it as one of the very first public figures to break the taboo about alcoholism in Ireland.

Eddie Keher (1941–), Kilkenny

Kilkenny has been blessed by the presence of some of the most stylish hurlers of all time – Lory Meagher, Paddy Phelan, Jim Langton and DJ Carey among them – but Eddie Keher was probably the greatest of them all.

From the Rower/Inistioge club, Keher was considered a prodigy during his four years playing at minor level. In 1959, at the age of eighteen, came a historic achievement when he played in the All-Ireland senior and minor hurling finals. The senior final against Waterford ended in a draw and Keher was again drafted onto the senior team for the replay. He acquitted himself well, even though Kilkenny lost. Four years later he finally won his first All-Ireland medal, scoring 0-14 as his county avenged their 1959 defeat by Waterford.

Keher, an exceptionally skilful hurler who has probably never been equalled for consistent accuracy, picked up winner's medals in 1967 and 1969, but his greatest displays came in the 1971–1975 period when the Black and Amber reached five All-Ireland finals in a row.

In 1971 Keher set a new All-Ireland final scoring record when he scored 2-11 as Kilkenny lost to Tipperary. The following year he scored 2-6, his two goals coming in the second half as a remarkable revival saw Kilkenny trip up Cork to win by seven points. He had also scored 0-17 against Galway in the semi-final of that year.

Keher missed out on the 1973 All-Ireland final against Limerick through injury – one of several which cost Kilkenny dear on the day. But he hit 1-11 the following year when Kilkenny set the record straight by overwhelming Limerick in the final. And he was in equally deadly form the following year, racking up 2-7 as his side easily overcame Galway. Keher retired in 1977 after a career as one of the great marksmen of hurling.

The 1887 team, winners of the first All-Ireland hurling championship (photographed about 191?)

Back Row : D. Maher, J. Sullivan, E. Murphy, J. Ryan, M. Maher, E. Leamy, T. Burke, C. Callanan, D. Davoren, M. Maher.

Centre Row : P. Ryan, D. Maher, J. Stapleton (Capt.), T. Maher, G. Leamy, J. Ryan, J. Dwyer

Front Row : M. Carroll, M. McNamara, T. Butler.

15. A BRIEF HISTORY OF THE ALL-IRELAND HURLING CHAMPIONSHIPS

From the outset, the hurling championship was a much more exclusive affair than the football championship. Nineteen counties have won the football championship; thirteen have won the hurling championship. Three of those titles belong to Kerry (1891), London (1901) and Laois (1915), none of whom are serious contenders these days. But the really telling statistic is that, between them, three counties have won eighty-one of the 116 hurling championships contested to date. Cork, Tipperary and Kilkenny are the undisputed Big Three of hurling and their domination has lasted from the beginning of the hurling championships to the present day.

Another difference between the football and hurling championships is the number of counties which contest them. Every county except Kilkenny competes in the All-Ireland football competition, whereas only about half of the Association's counties participate in the hurling equivalent. Galway are the only competitors from Connacht, while just three of Ulster's nine counties take part (Down, Derry and Antrim), although New York and London occasionally make a token appearance in that province's championship. In Leinster, only Kilkenny, Wexford and Offaly enter the championship with any hope of honours.

The Big Three didn't waste much time establishing their superiority. Tipperary won the very first hurling final, while it fell to Cork to win the game's first three-in-a-row, triumphing from 1892 to 1894. Two of those winning teams came from the Blackrock hurling club in Cork City, which is still one of the strongest in the country. Cork were succeeded at the top, as would often happen, by Tipperary, specifically by the men from Tubberadora club, who were regarded as the finest team of hurling's early days.

Unlike Blackrock, the Tubberadora club became extinct, though the area, in the Boherlahan–Dualla parish, remained a hurling hotbed. They won finals in 1895, 1896 and 1898, captained on each occasion by the famed Mikey Maher, memorably described by the great GAA journalist PD Mehigan, aka Carbery, as 'a thundering man, six feet two and fifteen stone hard-trained.' Maher also played for the Tipperary teams from Moycarkey and Twomileborris, which won the 1899 and 1900 finals respectively and gave the Premier County its first three-in-a-row.

Two pieces of the triptych were now in place and Kilkenny got in on the act with wins in 1904, 1905 and 1907. The 1907 final, in which they beat Cork by 3-12 to 4-8 at Fraher's Field in Dungarvan, County Waterford, was regarded as the best hurling match yet seen. A record attendance of 15,000 attended and watched a Kilkenny team that included such legends as Dick 'Drug' Walsh and Matt Gargan win with a late point from Jack Anthony. Between 1900 and 1909 the Big Three won nine of the ten titles on offer, a clean sweep being avoided by London's win over Cork in 1901. A pattern that was to become very familiar had been established.

Kilkenny put together another three-in-a-row between 1911 and 1913, although that decade was more notable for some historic breakthroughs. Wexford won their first title in 1910 with a 7-0 to 6-2 win over Limerick. In 1914 Clare had their first final victory, 5-1 to 1-0 over Laois. And a year later Laois won their first, and to date only, hurling title with an upset seven-point win over Cork. But from 1914 to 1928 no team was able to dominate, and no team managed to win successive titles.

Limerick became the first team to win the Liam McCarthy Cup when they beat Dublin 8-5 to 3-2 in the 1921 final, played two years late because of the Civil War. Perhaps the most notable victory of this period was Galway's first All-Ireland win, in 1923, when they beat Limerick by 7-3 to 4-5 with a team inspired by the brilliant Mick Gill of Ballinderreen at midfield. When Galway played Dublin in the 1924 final, Gill was playing with the Dubs – he had migrated to the capital in the interim – and once more ended up on the winning side. Dublin also won in 1927 with a side which had the unusual distinction of not having a single player native to the city: in addition to Gill, there were five players from Clare, three from Laois, and two each from Tipperary, Kilkenny and Limerick. Many of them were members of the Gardaí who had been transferred to Dublin to work there. However, in the following year a rule allowing players living in Dublin to play with their home counties came into force, and more or less ended the capital city's status as a hurling power.

It was the late 1920s before a team emerged to dominate hurling. The great Cork team of that era won All-Irelands in 1926, 1928, 1929 and 1931, the last of these victories coming after three games which captured the national imagination as no hurling matches had before. The Cork team was dominated by players from the Blackrock club, the greatest of whom were Eugene 'Eudie' Coughlan, Paddy 'Balty' Aherne and Michael 'Gah' Ahearne. They also had Dinny Barry-Murphy of the Éire Óg club, an exceptional wing-back. In 1928 they defeated Galway by twenty-seven points, a record-winning margin in a final, which would be equalled in 1944 but never surpassed. Gah Ahearne's 5-4 in that final remains the record individual score in a hurling final.

But it was the 1931 final which guaranteed immortality to this Cork team, and also to the Kilkenny side which eventually lost to them in a second replay. The saga began with a 1-6 draw, Eudie Coughlan getting a late equalising point for Cork to force the replay. That replay is still considered one of the greatest matches ever played and still occurs as a topic of heated debate and discussion in Munster pubs. It finished 2-5 apiece, with Cork once more coming from behind to draw. By now the finals had inspired great interest and a proposal was made at Central Council that the two counties be declared joint champions. The motion was defeated 10-6, and the old rivals were scheduled to meet one more time.

Unfortunately for Kilkenny, their captain and star player, Lory Meagher, wasn't able to play in the second replay due to a rib injury and this loss seemed to knock the stuffing out of them. Cork won 5-8 to 3-4. It was a last hurrah for that great team, who would lose their star player shortly afterwards. Up to that point, the Blackrock club alone had selected the Cork team, but when the County Board elected to change this, Eudie Coughlan retired from inter-county hurling in protest. Other Blackrock players followed his lead and Cork hurling entered the doldrums for a while.

In their absence two teams dominated the decade. The Kilkenny team, inspired by Meagher who was perhaps the best midfielder of all time, won All-Irelands in 1932, 1934 and 1935. The 1933 and 1935 final victories were at the expense of a hugely exciting Limerick team that included the inimitable Mick Mackey. His Limerick side won the 1934, 1936 and 1940 All-Irelands and their swashbuckling style of play was largely responsible for a huge upsurge of interest in hurling nationally.

The expectation that surrounded the 1933 final between these two great teams can be gauged by the fact that the game drew 45,000 fans – the biggest ever for a sporting event in Ireland up to that time. Another 5,000 fans were locked outside the Croke Park gates to avoid overcrowding and missed the sight of Johnny Dunne scoring a great goal late in the game to give Kilkenny a 1-7 to 0-6 win. The following year Dublin disposed of Kilkenny in the Leinster championship and met Limerick in the final. The first match was a draw, but in the replay a remarkable four-goal haul from Dave Clohessy gave Limerick a 5-2 to 2-6 victory.

There was another huge crowd for part two of Limerick versus Kilkenny in 1935. Mackey was at the height of his powers and Limerick had been regal in their progress through Munster. Unexpectedly, the hot favourites lost by 2-5 to 2-4, with Mackey being denied in the last minute by defender Paddy Larkin, whose son Fan and grandson Philly would also win All-Ireland medals with Kilkenny.

It was Limerick who had the final word in one of the game's greatest rivalries. They were probably at their absolute peak in 1936 and Mackey had been unstoppable all year, scoring an incredible 5-3 in the Munster final against Tipperary. Even Kilkenny were no match for them in an All-Ireland decider which Limerick won by 5-6 to 1-5.

Cork returned to the limelight in 1939 when they played Kilkenny in what has become known as the 'thunder and lightning' final. The weather gods were displaying an appetite for symbolism: the Second World War had begun two days earlier. In another classic encounter, Kilkenny confirmed their status as the kings of narrow victories when a last-minute Jimmy Kelly point gave them a 2-7 to 3-3 victory over Cork.

The following year was notable for the renaissance of a Limerick team widely considered too old to win. Mackey rallied his men for one final assault on Croke Park and, fittingly, it was Kilkenny who provided the opposition. The Leinster champions were leading by 1-6 to 1-2 early in the second half when Mackey moved out to midfield from centre half-forward and proceeded to turn the game Limerick's way. They emerged as 3-7 to 1-7 winners – a fitting coda to the story of a team that included, along with Mackey, such all-time greats as Paddy Scanlan, Paddy Clohessy, Timmy Ryan and Jackie Power.

Since their 1931 victory, Cork had gone nine years without winning an All-Ireland, but they were to atone for this in some style by becoming the only county to win four All-Irelands in a row, from 1941 to 1944. There was a touch of good fortune about their first victory as both Tipperary and Kilkenny were forced to withdraw from the championship because of an outbreak of foot-and-mouth disease in those counties. Cork's 5-11 to 0-6 victory over Dublin in the final may have had a hollow ring to it, but they would subsequently prove themselves as worthy champions.

In 1942 they defeated Tipperary en route to meeting Dublin in another final, which they won by 2-13 to 3-4. And the following year they became the first team in thirty years to complete a three-in-a-row, although their opposition in the final was completely unexpected. Antrim were partaking in the senior championship only because the junior championship had been suspended due to wartime travel restrictions. As a result, their 3-3 to 1-6 semi-final win over Kilkenny in Belfast ranks as maybe the greatest shock in the history of the GAA. A forewarned and forearmed Cork showed no mercy in the final, winning by a record-equalling margin of twenty-seven points.

Cork's four-in-a-row campaign was their toughest yet. It took two games to beat Limerick in the Munster final and they edged Galway out in the All-Ireland semi-final by just one point. The All-Ireland final was probably their easiest game, with Irish sprint champion Joe Kelly starring at corner-forward as they beat Dublin 2-13 to 1-2.

Cork's victory run finally came to a halt in 1945, but in the 1946 final they hammered Kilkenny 7-5 to 3-8. The man of the match was Christy Ring, who scored a goal just before half-time which is regarded as perhaps the best ever in an All-Ireland final. Ring was irresistible and from that time his exploits meant he was regarded as the undisputed greatest hurler of all time. No Irish sportsman has been regarded with such awe and admiration as Ring, and his is the star which shines brightest when the history of the GAA is reviewed.

Yet Kilkenny reined him in in 1947 when they once more squeaked through in a tight finish, two late Terry Leahy points giving them a 0-14 to 2-7 win over Cork. A year later Kilkenny's neighbours, Waterford, made history when they won their first All-Ireland by defeating Dublin 6-7 to 4-2, with the incredibly talented John Keane starring at centre half-forward.

The period from 1949 to 1954 saw Cork and Tipperary completely dominate hurling as two of the finest teams to play the game went head to head in Munster, in contests of such excellence that they even overshadowed the All-Ireland finals.

Tipperary had the upper hand initially, getting the ball rolling in 1949 with a win over Cork in extra time in an epic first-round replay. Over two games corner-back Tommy Doyle from Thurles didn't allow Christy Ring a single score from play. By comparison, the All-Ireland final was child's play. Around 67,000 fans thronged Croke Park to see if Laois, playing in their first final for thirty-four years, could spring another upset. They couldn't. Tipperary romped home by 3-11 to 0-3.

The following year saw Tipp beat Cork in the Munster final after a game marred by crowd disturbances that culminated in Tipperary goalkeeper, Tony Reddan, having to be smuggled out of the ground by a group of priests, for his own safety. The All-Ireland final was a much closer game than the previous year's and it took a late Paddy Kenny goal to see Tipperary past Kilkenny on a 1-9 to 1-8 scoreline. Tipp went for their first three-in-a-row in fifty-one years the following season. Despite a bravura performance from Ring, the champions held onto their Munster crown, winning a final for the ages, 2-11 to 2-9. Their opponents in the All-Ireland were Wexford, playing in their first decider since 1918. Tipperary completed their three-in-a-row with a resounding 7-7 to 3-9 victory.

Their hopes of a four-in-a-row came unstuck in the 1952 Munster final when a Ring-inspired Cork team won by 1-11 to 2-7. Now it was Cork's turn to dominate, and they swept Dublin aside 2-14 to 0-7 in the All-Ireland final.

The following year they once again beat Tipperary in the Munster final and a record crowd of 71,195 were there to see them take on Galway in what was probably the dirtiest final ever played. Cork won 3-3 to 0-8, but the major talking point was the damaged jaw and broken teeth suffered by Galway captain Mickey Burke. Burke had been marking Ring, who eventually tired of his attentions and struck him with his hurley. The Galway players were incensed and that night attacked Ring in the Gresham Hotel in Dublin. Ring escaped, but the following day the Galway men looked for more retribution, and seven of them again went for Ring as he ate breakfast, now in Barry's Hotel. The Cork players hit back to defend their star, and the subsequent fracas saw Cork manager Jim Barry attempting to break down the door behind which the Galway men were hiding from the irate Cork team. It had been a festival of ill feeling.

Tipperary once more suffered a narrow defeat by Cork in 1954 and, as had been the case three years previously, Wexford stood between the Munster champions and three titles in a row. But this was a very different side from the callow outfit of 1951. Wexford had been awesome on their way to the final, scoring 25-33 in three games and conceding just 3-14. Their full-forward, Nicky Rackard, had scored 5-4 in the Leinster final and 6-6 in the All-Ireland semi-final. A record 84,000-strong crowd thronged Croke Park in anticipation of a shooting match between Ring and Rackard.

It didn't happen that way, but the match was a classic encounter nonetheless. Wexford lost their brilliant full-back Nick O'Donnell early in the second half – he retired with a broken collar bone – but Bobby Rackard, Nicky's brother, played the game of his life when switched to the edge of the square. Nicky Rackard and Ring were both well tamed, and Wexford led all the way until a late goal from Johnny Clifford enabled Cork to win 1-9 to 1-6.

It was heartbreaking for the Slaneysiders – certainly one of the most charismatic teams in the history of hurling – but they finally ended their forty-five-year wait when they beat Galway

3-13 to 2-8 in the 1955 final. Cork had been knocked out of the Munster championship by Clare, but they were back in 1956 and faced up to Wexford in a final for the second time in three years. This time it was Wexford who came out on top, inspired by a great save by keeper Art Foley late in the game, which denied Ring a vital score. The save was followed by a sweeping Wexford move that gave Nicky Rackard the chance to score the clinching goal in a nail-biting 2-14 to 2-8 victory.

There was a notable revival in 1959 when Waterford won their second, and to date last, All-Ireland with an exciting 3-12 to 1-10 over their neighbours, Kilkenny, who had beaten them by a point in the final two years previously. But no one knew then that the game was about to be taken over by a side which has good claims to being the most powerful ever.

Tipperary won All-Ireland finals in 1961, 1962, 1964 and 1965 – the last two by huge margins. By the end of their reign they were dominating the game to an extent that had rarely been seen before, and had it not been for a defeat by Waterford in the 1963 Munster final they would have won an unprecedented five-in-a-row. They had no obvious weaknesses, but there were two players who really stood out. Although not related, they bore the same surname: Doyle. John of Holycross was the toughest and most accomplished defender of his day, who would eventually equal Ring's record of eight All-Ireland winner's medals; Jimmy of Thurles was one of the game's most skilled forwards.

Their run of final victories began tentatively. Tipp were red-hot favourites against Dublin in 1961, but only squeezed through by 0-16 to 1-12. What made that all-important margin of difference between the two teams was Liam Devaney's performance when moved to centre half-back. The 1962 final, however, was a tremendous match, which began with Tipp scoring two goals in the first ninety seconds through Tom Moloughney and Sean McLoughlin, leaving the crowd almost speechless. An aging Wexford team fought back courageously and had actually moved two points clear with thirteen minutes left, but a goal from Tom Ryan of Killenaule put Tipperary back in front and they went on to win 3-10 to 2-11.

Over-confidence seemed responsible for Tipperary's defeat in 1963 when Waterford beat them in the Munster final, but they brooked no resistance in the following two championships. In the 1964 final they destroyed reigning All-Ireland champions Kilkenny 5-13 to 2-8, with Donie Nealon scoring three goals and Jimmy Doyle putting ten points on the board. And the following year Wexford were put to the sword 2-16 to 0-10. The closest any team came to them in those two campaigns was twelve points.

The Cork team that won the 1966 final was not in the same class as the great Tipperary sides of that era, but their 3-9 to 1-10 victory over Kilkenny took place on one of the most emotional of September Sundays. It had been twelve years since a Cork team had even reached a final – an unthinkable gap for one of the Big Three – and their young team was not fancied to beat a far more experienced Kilkenny side. But thanks to Colm Sheehan scoring two goals, Cork won through by sheer dint of effort, ending the famine that had scourged them for so long.

Three years later it was Cork's turn to be favourites and Kilkenny's to do the upsetting. Kilkenny won 2-15 to 2-9 with a superb performance from Eddie Keher, unquestionably one of the finest attackers of all time. This win was by way of a prologue to a golden period for Kilkenny hurling. They contested every final between 1971 and 1975, winning three, and save for some bad luck with injuries could certainly have won at least four in a row.

They began with a loss in the highest scoring All-Ireland final to date. Playing time had been increased to eighty minutes and both Tipperary and Kilkenny made the most of those extra minutes. Tipp won by 5-17 to 5-14; Keher ended on the losing side despite a record-breaking haul of 2-11.

Defeat looked to be Kilkenny's fate again when they trailed by eight points with twenty minutes left of the 1972 final against Cork. There then followed the greatest comeback in final history as the Cats scored 2-9 without reply to win by 3-24 to 5-11. Keher was rampant again and started the revival with a great goal from a 21-yard free, while the second goal in the revival came from Frank Cummins, the wonderful midfielder who played his club hurling for Blackrock in Cork.

Nobody begrudged Limerick their 1973 All-Ireland title as it had been thirty-three years since their last victory, but Kilkenny were without Keher and three other first-team players and looked only a pale shadow of themselves in a 1-21 to 1-14 defeat. They seemed to make a point in the following year's final with a 3-19 to 1-13 victory, to which Keher contributed 1-11. And a thumping 2-22 to 2-10 victory over Galway in 1975 completed the memorable exploits of perhaps the greatest Kilkenny team of all.

Great and all as they had been, Kilkenny hadn't been able to win three in a row. But the Cork team which succeeded them did just that, getting the run underway with an immensely exciting 2-21 to 4-11 win over a Wexford team that had led by eight points early in the game. Cork had an array of talented forwards to call on, including a couple of all-time greats in Jimmy Barry-Murphy and Ray Cummins, as well as Seanie O'Leary, one of the finest goal-poachers the game has known. It was an O'Leary goal that proved vital in 1977 when Cork once more got the better of Wexford, this time by 1-17 to 3-8. Kilkenny stood between Cork and a three-in-a-row the following year, but Cork won easily enough, 1-15 to 2-8, with Barry-Murphy scoring the crucial goal. The achievement of that 1976–1978 Cork team looks even more impressive in retrospect as there has been no three-in-a-row since.

The 1966 final may have been an emotional occasion, but it was knocked into a cocked hat by the 1980 decider. In fact, the celebrations following Galway's 2-15 to 3-9 victory over

Limerick were arguably the most joyous ever seen in Croke Park. Galway hadn't won a championship since 1923, but they jumped into an early lead with goals from Bernie Forde and PJ Molloy and held on tightly as Limerick mounted a ferocious fightback. The day belonged to Galway, however, as they proved they had the big match temperament. The scenes at the end were memorable, with captain Joe Connolly declaring, in imitation of the Pope, 'People of Galway, we love you,' and Joe McDonagh, who would later become President of the GAA, giving a heartfelt rendition of 'The West's Awake'.

A year later came an even more remarkable victory. For years Offaly had been whipping boys in Leinster and were not considered as a hurling power at all. But in 1980 they shocked everyone by beating Kilkenny in the Leinster final. The following year they proved to have staying power by defeating Wexford in the provincial decider. Nonetheless, they were outsiders against Galway in the final and trailed by seven points early in the second half. Then began a great comeback, inspired by centre half-back Pat Delaney, which ended with a 2-12 to 0-15 Offaly victory. The crucial score was a goal five minutes from the end by veteran corner-forward Johnny Flaherty. It was a remarkable achievement as it had been thirty-three years since a new county had won a hurling All-Ireland, and there have been no first-time victors since. Offaly built on this success and have been one of the top counties ever since.

They were succeeded by a fine Kilkenny team who defeated Cork convincingly in the 1982 final and narrowly in the 1983 final. Giant full-forward Christy Heffernan scored two goals and generally went on the rampage against the Cork defence in the 3-18 to 1-13 win first time round, while Billy Fitzpatrick proved himself a worthy heir to Eddie Keher by scoring ten points in the final the following year.

The late 1980s saw Galway produce their finest ever team, although initially they were regarded as 'chokers' on big match days following narrow defeats in the 1985 and 1986 finals. They laid any doubts about their character to rest in 1987 when they defeated Kilkenny 1-12 to 0-9 in a grimly physical and mostly unenjoyable final. But they showed signs of greatness the following year with a thrilling 1-15 to 0-14 victory over Tipperary in the final – Noel Lane scoring the only goal of the game, as he had the previous year.

The Galway–Tipperary rivalry defined their era. It began when the Westerners had beaten Tipp 3-20 to 2-17 in the 1987 semi-final, followed by another convincing win in 1988, which suggested the Galwegians had the edge on their southern neighbours. The following year, however, saw one of the most bitter controversies in the history of hurling when Galway's star centre half-back, Tony Keady, was suspended for playing illegally in a hurling match in America. It was bad enough that Keady had been reported by a Tipperary man, but there was also a widespread belief that his punishment did not fit his crime and was too harsh by far. Galway threatened to withdraw from the championship, but eventually agreed to play Tipperary in the semi-final – without Keady. It was a bitter encounter, and Galway had two men sent off as they lost by three points.

It had been an unsatisfactory way for great champions to be dethroned, but Tipperary's return to the top was a welcome one. Amazingly, they had not won a single Munster title from 1972 to 1986, so their 1987 Munster final win over Cork was greeted with a jubilation that few All-Ireland victories had produced. On top of that, they had a charismatic manager in Michael 'Babs' Keating and two sublime forwards in Nicky English and Pat Fox. They stormed into the 1989 competition, where they would meet unusual opposition in the final.

Since Antrim's thrashing by Cork in 1944 times had been lean for Ulster hurling. A couple of brave semi-final performances by the Antrim team indicated that the standard in the province was rising, but no one expected them to defeat Offaly 4-15 to 1-15 and advance to a final meeting with

Tipperary. Sadly, the fairytale ended there as Tipperary walloped Antrim by 4-24 to 3-9 and Nicky English amassed a total of 2-12 in the process. Tipp's eighteen-point winning margin that day was the largest since 1944.

If the 1989 final had been too one-sided for enjoyment, the following year's final certainly made up for it. The two finalists, Cork and Galway, swapped scores at a furious rate: forty-three in seventy minutes. Joe Cooney, Galway's great centre half-forward, was unstoppable in the first half and led his team to a five-point half-time lead. But Cork's ability to steal goals kept them in the game, and a tremendous solo goal by Tomás Mulcahy finally turned the game their way. It ended 5-15 to 2-21 for Cork, and there have been few better finals in the history of the competition.

The fine Tipperary team won their second title in 1991 when they defeated Kilkenny 1-16 to 0-15, but a battling performance by a young Kilkenny team in defeat heralded that county's return to pre-eminence. They beat Cork by 3-10 to 1-12 in 1992 and had five points to spare over Galway the following year. Kilkenny's first goal in 1992 came from a young wing-forward named DJ Carey, who soon became recognised as the best hurler of the modern era, a forward with pace, skill and a flair for the spectacular which led some people to claim that he was the best since Ring.

The 1990s was a remarkable hurling decade where the out-of-the-ordinary was the norm. Take the finish of the 1994 final, for example. Limerick were five points clear with five minutes left only for Offaly to score 2-5 without reply and win 3-16 to 2-13. But the real miracle was the revival of Clare under Ger Loughnane, perhaps the most controversial, outspoken and brilliant manager the game of hurling has ever known.

Two Munster final drubbings in 1993 and 1994 had reduced the stock of Clare hurling almost to zero when Loughnane took over. Players such as full-back Brian Lohan

and centre half-back Sean McMahon would become house-
hold names, but they were unranked unknowns as Clare
embarked on what was to be an incredible championship
campaign in 1995. Outsiders in every single game they
played, they overcame Cork and then Limerick to win their
first Munster title in sixty-three years. A semi-final win over
Galway gave them an All-Ireland final date with a heavily fancied Offaly side.

Clare stuck with Offaly all the way, but trailed by 2-7 to
0-11 with four minutes left to play. Then sub Eamonn Taafe
scored a last-minute goal and Anthony Daly struck an inspirational 65 over the bar to let Clare win by 1-13 to 2-8. It was
their first All-Ireland victory in eighty-one years and the Clare
fans were, understandably, completely overwhelmed by the
occasion. Few Irish sporting victories have struck such a
chord with the general public: the Clare men defined the true
meaning of perseverance.

The following year, 1996, was pretty special too. Another
colourful manager, Liam Griffin, led Wexford to their first All-
Ireland title in twenty-eight years when they defeated Limerick 1-13 to 0-14 in the final. The following year Clare returned
and proved that 1995 was not a once-off. They had the enviable and laudable distinction of beating each of the Big Three
on the way to the final, and for good measure they beat Tipperary a second time in the final (this was the first year of the
back-door system in hurling). In a tremendously exciting
finish, superb late points from Ollie Baker and Jamesie O'Connor gave Clare a 0-20 to 2-13 victory.

Clare were red-hot favourites to make it three championships in four years, but they went astray in the strange year of
1998. A rough Munster final replay against Waterford produced two sendings-off and a long suspension for Clare midfielder Colin Lynch. Convinced they had been badly treated
by GAA authorities over-reacting to public pressure, Clare
retreated into a siege mentality, and Loughnane, whether he

meant to or not, stoked the fire with some ill-advised comments he made in interviews with the media. By the time they met Offaly in Dublin for the semi-final, tensions were running very high indeed. Clare built up a big early lead, but Offaly closed the gap in the final quarter. With Clare leading by three points, referee Jimmy Cooney mistakenly blew for time two minutes early. Offaly fans occupied the Croke Park pitch in protest, and the GAA ordered a second replay. Offaly won this one and beat Kilkenny, who'd beaten them in Leinster, in the finals.

Five years in a row the Liam McCarthy Cup had gone to counties outside the Big Three. It was an unprecedented run, but it was not to last. Cork won their first All-Ireland in nine years in 1999, and Tipp their first in ten years in 2001, but it was Kilkenny who dominated. They beat Offaly in the 2000 final, with DJ Carey giving a devastating performance, and the great attacker excelled again two years later when they defeated Clare. In 2003 Kilkenny became the first team in ten years to win two hurling All-Irelands in a row when they defeated Cork 1-14 to 1-11. Despite the rebellions of the 1990s, the old aristocracy was still ensconced in the big house.

Number of All-Ireland hurling titles held by the winning counties:

28 – Cork, Kilkenny

25 – Tipperary

7 – Limerick

6 – Dublin, Wexford

4 – Galway, Offaly

3 – Clare

2 – Waterford

1 – Kerry, Laois, London

16. THE ALL-STARS

Since the 1960s there had been a tradition of annually select-
ing the best player in each position, in football and hurling, to
create a special team of the year. From 1963 to 1967 the top
players in each position were named in the Cú Chulainn
Awards and played together in the Cardinal Cushing tourna-
ment, a now defunct competition.

A new era was ushered in in 1971 when this 'fantasy team'
selection was formalised into the annual All-Star Awards. The
All-Stars team comprises the best player in each position,
regardless of club or county affiliation; together, they form a
formidable team. Thanks to sponsorship from the PJ Carroll
tobacco company of Dundalk, the All-Star teams of the 1970s
were able to tour America and play a series of exhibition
games against the All-Ireland champions of the year. The first
tour saw two games played in San Francisco, and other Ameri-
can cities came on board later. It was a great honour to be
selected as an All-Star as it bestowed on those chosen the title
of Best Player in their position – a distinction not to be sniffed
at in such highly competitive sports.

The initial sponsors fell foul of the clamp-down on ciga-
rette advertising and were replaced in 1978 by Bank of Ireland. The USA tours ended in the mid-1980s, although the
All-Stars did play in Toronto in 1990 and 1991. Powerscreen
took over the sponsorship for a couple of years in the 1990s,
before being replaced by Eircell, the company now known as
Vodafone. Under Vodafone's sponsorship the trips abroad
and exhibition games have been revived, with exotic loca-
tions, such as Dubai, taking the place of America.

Two players share the distinction of having won nine All-
Star awards apiece: Pat Spillane of Kerry in football, and DJ
Carey of Kilkenny in hurling. A unique record is held by Ray
Cummins of Cork who won awards in the same year, 1971, in

both football and hurling. Three other players, Jimmy Barry-Murphy, Brian Murphy of Cork and Liam Currams of Offaly, have also won dual football and hurling awards. The increasing demands of the modern game make it unlikely that their feat, let alone that of Cummins, will be emulated again.

Five father-and-son pairings have won All-Stars. Four of these were in football: Pat (1971) and Paddy (1999) Reynolds of Meath; Dermot (1974, 1979) and Dermot (1998) Earley of Roscommon and Kildare respectively; Liam (1973) and Kevin (1998) O'Neill of Galway and Mayo respectively; and Frank (1984) and Brian (2003) McGuigan of Tyrone. The only hurling father-and-son duo is that of Fan (1973, 1974, 1976, 1978) and Philly (2002) Larkin of Kilkenny.

To continue the family theme, there are three sets of three brothers who have won All-Stars: Billy, Joe and Johnny Dooley of Offaly hurlers; Pat, Ger and John Henderson of Kilkenny hurlers; and Pat, Tom and Mick Spillane of Kerry footballers. Kerry have won more football All-Stars than any other county, while Kilkenny are on top in hurling All-Stars. Longford, Carlow and Louth have never been awarded an All-Star.

Perhaps the most famous (or infamous, depending on your viewpoint) All-Star moment was the decision in 1994 to omit Brian Whelehan of Offaly from the hurling team and give his place instead to Dave Clarke of Limerick, a good player who nevertheless had nothing like as impressive a season as Whelehan had enjoyed. The ensuing furore culminated in a decision to change the way the team was selected. For many years the All-Stars team was selected by the votes of all the country's GAA journalists, today it is selected by a much smaller panel of journalists from the national media.

The players named most often in each All-Star position are:

Football

Goalkeeper: John O'Leary (Dublin), 5.

Right corner-back: Harry Keegan (Roscommon), 3, Robbie O'Malley (Meath), Páidí Ó Sé (Kerry), 3.

Full-back: John O'Keefe (Kerry), 4.

Left corner-back: Robbie Kelleher (Dublin), 4.

Right half-back: Tommy Drumm (Dublin), Tommy Doyle (Kerry), 3.

Centre half-back: Tom Spillane (Kerry), Kieran McGeeney (Armagh), 3.

Left half-back: Martin O'Connell (Meath), 3.

Midfield: Jack O'Shea (Kerry), 6, Darragh Ó Sé (Kerry), John McDermott (Meath), Anthony Tohill (Derry), 3.

Right half-forward: Ger Power (Kerry), Barney Rock (Dublin), 3.

Centre half-forward: Larry Tompkins (Cork), Trevor Giles (Meath), 3.

Left half-forward: Pat Spillane (Kerry), 8.

Right corner-forward: Mike Sheehy (Kerry), 6.

Full-forward: Peter Canavan (Tyrone), 4.

Left corner-forward: John Egan (Kerry), 4.

Hurling

Goalkeeper: Noel Skehan (Kilkenny), 6.

Right corner-back: Fan Larkin (Kilkenny), 4.

Full-back: Pat Hartigan (Limerick), 5.

Left corner-back: Martin Hanamy (Offaly), John Horgan (Cork), 3.

Right half-back: Peter Finnerty (Galway), 5.

Centre half-back: Ger Henderson (Kilkenny), 5.

Left half-back: Denis Coughlan (Cork), Iggy Clarke (Galway), 3.

Midfield: John Fenton (Cork), 5, Frank Cummins (Kilkenny), 4.

Right half-forward: Nicky English (Tipperary), 3.

Centre half-forward: Joe Cooney (Galway), Gary Kirby (Limerick), Martin Quigley (Wexford), 3.

Left half-forward: Seven players with two awards each.

Right full-forward: Pat Fox (Tipperary), Charlie McCarthy (Cork), Mick Brennan (Kilkenny), 3.

Full-forward: Joe McKenna (Limerick), 4.

Left full-forward: DJ Carey (Kilkenny), Eddie Keher (Kilkenny), Liam Fennelly (Kilkenny), Seanie O'Leary (Cork), Eamonn Cregan (Limerick), 3.

17. THE VOICE OF THE GAA: MICHEÁL O'HEHIR

Better known than most players and better loved than any other media figure, Micheál O'Hehir achieved an incredible prominence as the finest commentator the games ever had. He became known as the voice of the GAA during nearly fifty years of commentating for RTÉ radio and television.

It's not surprising that O'Hehir was such a brilliant commentator when one considers his background. He was steeped in the GAA from an early age, his father, Jim, having trained his native Clare to an All-Ireland hurling victory in 1914. As a schoolboy, O'Hehir first listened to a commentary on a game when he was lying sick in bed one day. He wrote to RTÉ seeking an audition, and made his debut while still a teenager in 1938, commentating on the All-Ireland football semi-final between Galway and Monaghan.

In the days before television, and when travel was more difficult than it is now, O'Hehir was the only link many people had with the big championship games of the day. Communities would gather in houses to listen to the crystal radio sets of the day, and O'Hehir's evocative style made his the commentary they all wanted to hear.

His finest hour came when describing the 1947 All-Ireland final between Cavan and Kerry from the Polo Grounds, New York. It looked as though the phone-link to Ireland would be lost for the final minutes of the game, but O'Hehir pleaded and cajoled and the line was kept open and the audience back home got to hear the finish.

O'Hehir was also a fine commentator on other sports, most notably horse racing, but he will always be remembered for his contribution to the GAA. To this day many Irish commentators, consciously or not, ape his style, and when young lads in past decades kicked or pucked around a ball, it was always Micheál O'Hehir's commentary they heard in their head, describing their heroics.

18. CAMOGIE

Camogie is, to a large extent, the women's version of hurling. In 2004 the game celebrated its centenary – the first camogie association was founded in Dublin in 1904. However, the game really only came into its own after a special Congress in August 1932 in Dublin's Gresham Hotel, which codified rules, arranged for the first All-Ireland championships to be played for the O'Duffy Cup – presented by General Eoghan O'Duffy, famous as the founder of the Blueshirts, a right-wing movement which eventually became the Fine Gael party – and set up Cumann Camógaíochta na Gael (the Irish Camogie Association), the organisation that still runs the game and is affiliated to the GAA.

For many years one of the main differences between camogie and hurling was that the women's game was twelve-a-side and was played on a much smaller pitch. However, in 1999 the move was made to a fifteen-a-side game and a bigger pitch, something which was seen as a welcome move towards parity of esteem. Another distinguishing feature of camogie, as opposed to women's football, is that players must wear skirts rather than shorts – a slightly anachronistic nod to the sport's origins in an era with a more stereotypical idea of women.

Camogie's early years were badly disrupted by a controversy over whether men should be allowed to serve on the sport's committees. This led Cork to withdraw from the Association in 1944, with the Leinster counties following suit in 1945. It was 1951 before the stand-off was resolved and all the counties had returned to the fold.

Dublin won the 1932 All-Ireland championship and, although Cork put together a three-in-a-row between 1939 and 1941, the Dubs proceeded to dominate the game to a breathtaking extent. Between 1948 and 1966, they won eighteen of the nineteen titles on offer, with only an Antrim victory in 1956 breaking the sequence. This included a ten-in-a-row between 1957 and 1966, which is likely to remain a record, as is the achievement of Dublin's great midfielder, Kathleen Mills, in winning fifteen All-Ireland medals. Other outstanding members of those dominant Dublin teams were goalkeeper Eileen O'Duffy and full-forward Sophie Brack.

Antrim won the first title of the post-Dublin era, in 1967, but predictably enough it was the traditionally strong hurling counties who began to take over the competition from then on. Cork produced an outstanding team, which won four titles in a row from 1970 to 1973 and featured the brilliant defender Marie Costine. Costine played with the Killeagh club but was actually from Cloyne, home village of Christy Ring. In 1974 Kilkenny won their first ever All-Ireland with a team that included a teenage forward, Angela Downey, who would go on to become the nearest thing camogie has had to the legendary hurler, Christy Ring.

Downey, daughter of Shem Downey who won an All-Ireland hurling medal with Kilkenny in 1947, was totally unstoppable during her 1980s heyday. Skilful and athletic, she became the first camogie star to win widespread public recognition and did wonders for the image of the game, which had hitherto been somewhat looked down on by GAA afficionados. A famous goal where Downey continued attacking despite having had her skirt pulled off summed up her competitive instincts. She won twelve All-Ireland medals. The Kilkenny team that won seven in a row between 1985 and 1991 is regarded by many as the finest in the history of the game, with full-back Liz Neary, centre-back Bridie Martin and Downey's twin sister, Ann, also ranked among the greats.

Kilkenny were succeeded by a Cork team not far behind them in accomplishment, which won five of the seven titles available between 1992 and 1998 and starred Sandie Fitzgibbon, a product of the great Glen Rovers club (who, incidentally, also hold over sixty caps for Ireland at basketball). Galway won their first, and to date only, title in 1996. To date, just seven counties have won camogie All-Irelands: Dublin leads the way with twenty-six titles, followed by Cork with twenty. The other winners are Kilkenny, Tipperary, Antrim, Galway and Wexford, whose first title came in 1968.

It's odd that a county with the hurling tradition of Tipperary took so long to get in on the camogie act, but recently they've been making up for lost time. Their first All-Ireland title arrived with a 1999 win over Kilkenny, and they completed a three-in-a-row with victory over the same side in 2001. Cork dashed their hopes for four-in-a-row in 2002, but Tipp were back with a revenge win in 2003. Goalkeeper Jovita Delaney and full-forward Deirdre Hughes are perhaps the best-known players on a richly talented team that has the potential to equal and perhaps surpass the great sides of the past.

The centenary celebrations saw the naming of a team of the century (and controversy when Angela Downey refused to attend the celebration banquet because her sister hadn't been selected), and a feeling that camogie is a sport on the up and up. The crowds it draws are considerably less than those attracted to hurling, but interest, and media coverage, is increasing every year.

19. HANDBALL

Handball is the one game promoted by the GAA which possesses a genuine international dimension. The game, believed to have been spread by Irish emigrants, is played in the USA, Canada, Australia, Mexico and Spain.

The game was traditionally played in a four-wall alley, though there is a variant that uses just the front wall, and in the 40x20 game the roof is utilised as a fifth wall. Handball is played either between two players or between two doubles pairings of two. There are two alley sizes: 60x30 feet and 40x20 feet. The 60x30 form is the traditional game, but this has been surpassed in popularity by the newer version which spread to Ireland from the USA in the late 1960s.

Handball was originally played with a hardball, two inches in diameter and weighing an ounce-and-a-half, with a rubber centre bound in leather. But these days the softball – two-and-a-quarter inches in diameter, made out of rubber and weighing 62 grammes – is more popular. At senior level the first player to reach twenty-one points wins a game and the first player to win two games wins the match.

The Irish Handball Council was set up in 1924 and the two notable early stars of the game were JJ Gilmartin of Kilkenny and Pat Perry of Roscommon. Gilmartin had an extraordinary career, winning seven hardball titles in a row from 1936 to 1942, breaking his neck in a road accident in England and then coming back to win a three-in-a-row from 1945 to 1947. Perry won eight softball titles in a row from 1930 to 1937. The tradition exemplified by both men continues, with Kilkenny and Roscommon remaining among the strongest counties in handball; Cork and Clare are two other major powers.

The arrival of the 40x20 courts (the first one was built in

Oldtown, Dublin in 1969, with a further 152 built nationwide between 1973 and 1980) gave the game a huge boost. Not only were they indoor courts – a huge bonus given the Irish weather – but the smaller dimensions made for a faster and more exciting game. In terms of media interest, the 1970s were a golden age for the game in Ireland. RTÉ's 'Top Ace' programme, which began in 1973 and ran for nearly a decade, gave handball a huge public profile. Peadar McGee of Mayo emerged as the prime exponent of the hardball game, with six titles in a row between 1972 and 1977, but it was Pat Kirby of Clare who was the undisputed star of handball.

Kirby won the softball singles in the 60x30 court from 1974 to 1977 and took the 40x20 titles from 1975 to 1980, as well as winning the 'Top Ace' title on a number of occasions. His rivals, such as Dick Lyng of Wexford, Paddy Reilly of Kilkenny, Murty McEllistrim of Kerry, Jimmy Goggins of Wexford and Joe O'Brien of Roscommon, also spent time in the limelight.

From the 1980s onwards handball failed to receive the same level of media attention, but in that time it has produced arguably its greatest ever exponent of the game: Michael 'Duxie' Walsh of Kilkenny. Walsh won the 60x30 softball singles title thirteen times in a row from 1985 to 1997, as well as seven 40x20 titles. In 1994, 1995 and 1998 he won 40x20 doubles titles, partnered by none other than hurling legend DJ Carey, whose handball background often enables him to make particularly deft passes on the hurling field. Peter McAuley of Louth, a hardball expert, was the only player to seriously challenge Walsh for predominance in this period.

The first World Championships took place in 1964 and have generally been dominated by the Americans, which is why it was a notable landmark when, in October 2003, the first Irishman won a world singles title. Paul Brady of Cavan beat Tony Healy of Cork in an epic three-set final contest, and the fact that Fiona Shannon of Antrim won the women's singles title the same day indicates that handball in Ireland is still thriving.

APPENDIX

I. THE GAA COUNTY COLOURS

Antrim: yellow

Armagh: orange, white collars

Carlow: green, yellow and red thirds

Cavan: blue with white collars

Clare: gold and blue

Cork: red with white collars

Derry: white with red hoop

Donegal: yellow, green sleeves and collars

Down: red with black collars and sleeves

Dublin: sky blue

Fermanagh: green and white

Galway: maroon with white collars

Kerry: green with gold hoop

Kildare: all white

Kilkenny: black and amber stripes

Laois: blue with white hoop

Leitrim: green with gold hoop and white collars

Limerick: green, white collars

Longford: blue, yellow collars

Louth: red, white collars

Meath: green with gold collars and cuffs

Mayo: green with red hoop

Monaghan: white, blue collars

Offaly: Green, white and gold thirds

Roscommon: yellow with blue collars

Sligo: all black

Tyrone: white with red collars

Tipperary: blue with gold hoop

Waterford: white with blue collars

Westmeath: naroon with white collars

Wexford: purple with yellow shoulders

Wicklow: blue with gold stripe on sleeves

II. COMMON TEAM NICKNAMES

Clare: The Banner

Cork: The Rebels

Dublin: The Dubs

Galway: The Tribesmen

Kerry: The Kingdom

Kildare: The Lilywhites

Kilkenny: The Cats

Louth: The Wee County

Meath: The Royals

Offaly: The Faithful County

Roscommon: The Rossies

Tipperary: The Premier County

Waterford: The Decies

Wexford: The Yellowbellies

III. FAMOUS PLAYER NICKNAMES

Sean 'The Master' Purcell: Galway footballer, 1940s and 1950s.

John 'Tyler' Mackey: Limerick hurler, 1910s.

Des 'Snitchie' Ferguson: Dublin footballer and hurler, 1950s and 1960s.

Michael 'Babs' Keating: Tipperary hurler and footballer, 1960s and 1970s.

Phil 'The Gunner' Brady: Cavan footballer, 1940s and 1950s.

Paddy 'The Bawn' Brosnan: Kerry footballer, 1940s and 1950s.

Padraig 'The Flying Doctor' Carney: Mayo footballer, 1940s and 1950s.

John 'Tull' Dunne: Galway footballer, 1930s and 1940s.

Eugene 'Nudie' Hughes: Monaghan footballer, 1970s and 1980s.

Tim 'The Horse' Kennelly: Kerry footballer, 1970s and 1980s.

Martin 'The Wee Man' McHugh: Donegal footballer, 1980s and 1990s.

Tommy 'The Boy Wonder' Murphy: Laois footballer, 1930s and 1940s.

John Joe 'Goggles' Doyle: Clare hurler, 1920s and 1930s.

John 'Jobber' McGrath: Westmeath hurler, 1950s and 1960s.

Pa 'Fowler' McInerney: Clare hurler, 1920s and 1930s.

Terence 'Sambo' McNaughton: Antrim hurler, 1980s and 1990s.

Liam 'Chunky' O'Brien: Kilkenny hurler, 1970s.

Phil 'Fan' Larkin: Kilkenny hurler, 1960s and 1970s.

Jack 'Font' Fitzgerald: Kildare footballer, 1900s.

Pat 'Aeroplane' O'Shea: Kerry footballer, 1910s.

Pat 'Cocker' Daly: Dublin footballer, 1900s.

Bill 'Squires' Gannon: Kildare footballer, 1920s.